THE SONG OF
HIROSHIMA

by

ATSUHIRO OZAKI

W
wessex

THE SONG OF HIROSHIMA
by
ATSUHIRO OZAKI

EDITOR
NOEL CAPON

DESIGN / COVER DESIGN
ANNA BOTELHO

TRANSLATORS

SPANISH
ANDRÉS ROSENDE-NOVO

JAPANESE

CHOW TSZ CHING	KEN HONDA	MURAMATSU FUMIYA	MIO SHINDO	AYUKO MUELLER
周子静	本田健	村松文也	進藤美生	ミューラー　安遊子

CHINESE

ZONG YANGYANG	SIT WAI YIN	LIU XIAOCUI	YUAN LU
宗阳阳	薛慧妍	刘晓萃	袁璐

Printed in the USA

Library of Congress Cataloging-in-Publication Data

Ozaki, Atsuhiro
  The song of hiroshima / Atsuhiro Ozaki
    p. cm.
ISBN 978-0-9833300-0-4

Cataloging information is on file with the Library of Congress.

About WESSEX

Wessex publishes college- and graduate-level textbooks at significantly reduced prices compared to traditional publications — as printed books and as pdf e-books for downloading to the customer's computer. Customers may also reads Wessex's textbooks online for a free trial period, then *Pay What You Think It's Worth*. For information on *Fundamentals of International Business*, see **http://www.fib21c.com**. For information on *Managing Marketing in the 21st Century, Capon's Marketing Framework,* and *The Virgin Marketer*, see **http://www.axcesscapon.com**.

Wessex also publishes trade books like *Managing Global Accounts*,
see **http://www.wessex21c.com**.

You can learn more about activities related to Wessex at **http://www.axcesscapon.com**.

AXCESS
CAPON

TABLE OF CONTENTS
INDICE
目次
目录

PREFACE

by

NOEL CAPON

I N 1999, LOIS CREWS DIED AT AGE 94 IN PORT WASHINGTON, LONG ISLAND, NEW YORK. As my wife and I were Lois's closest relatives, and her house would be sold, it fell to Deanna and me to look through Lois's possessions, decide what to keep, and prepare the remainder for auction. While exploring the attic, I came across what appeared to be writing in a child's notebook. Some weeks later I read the notebook and now Wessex is publishing *The Song of Hiroshima*.

Before World War II, Lois's husband, Albert Crews, worked for NBC. After the war, as a member of General MacArthur's staff, he spent several weeks in Hiroshima advising personnel at the radio station. Albert received the handwritten notebook from Atsuhiro Ozaki, the secretary in charge of communications and translation.

On August 6, 1945, Mr. Ozaki was working at the radio station, less than 1,000 yards from where the atom bomb dropped. The notebook he delivered to Albert Crews describes what he did and what he saw during the next two to three days. In giving his notebook to Albert Crews, Mr. Ozaki wanted to share his experiences with people in the United States. We do not know if Albert ever used this material or whether the notebook just sat in the Port Washington attic for over half a century. Regardless, although 60 years have passed, this publication fulfills Atsuhiro Ozaki's wish.

In an effort to give this material wide circulation, Wessex is publishing *The Song of Hiroshima* in English, Spanish, Japanese, and Chinese languages. We also reproduce Atsuhiro Ozaki's letter to Albert Crews and his notebook in its entirety. In the published version, we have made minor spelling and other editorial changes to Mr. Ozaki's original text to aid in comprehension.

Noel Capon
Bronxville, New York
January 1, 2011

Noel Capon is the R.C. Kopf Professor of International Marketing, Columbia Business School, New York. Deanna Kuhn is Professor of Psychology and Education, Teachers College, Columbia University, New York.

Program Section
Hiroshima Central Broadcasting
Station, Hiroshima
March 27, '49

Dear Mr. Crews,

Pardon me my rudeness that I am going to write to you for the first time. I am a secretary in charge of communications and translation in our station. I know you came to this city at the middle of last month, and giving us good suggestions and direction about broadcasting job. Now if you mind, will you read my poorly done notes about the recollection of the first Atom bomb fell at Hiroshima which I have recently written and here I have enclosed. I have heard you are returning to the States next April. I am very glad, if you would use this material, when you speak and write about Japan over there. Anyhow I am glad if you have time to read my poor notes and take it to your country.

Yours Sincerely

A. Ozaki

P.S. Mr. Kodama of our station kindly take this letter and the notes to you.

Sección de Programación
Centro de emisiones Hiroshima
Emisora, Hiroshima
27 de marzo de 1949

Estimado Sr. Crews,

Perdone mi impertinencia al escribirle por primera vez. Soy el responsable de las comunicaciones y traducciones de nuestra emisora. Sé que usted vino a la ciudad a mediados del mes pasado y que nos ha dado buenas sugerencias y consejos sobre nuestras emisiones. Ahora, si no le molesta, me gustaría que leyese mis humildes notas sobre los acontecimientos que siguieron a la caída de la primera bomba atómica en Hiroshima y que adjunto con esta carta. He escuchado que regresa a los Estados Unidos el próximo abril y le estaría muy agradecido si utilizase este material cuando hable de Japón allí. En cualquier caso, le agradecería que leyese mis humildes notas, si tiene tiempo, y las lleve a su país.

Le saluda atentamente

A. Ozaki

P.D. El Sr. Kodama, de nuestra emisora, le lleva amablemente esta carta y notas a usted.

企画部
広島中央放送局
広島
1949年3月27日

拝啓
クルーズ様

初めてお手紙を出す無礼をお許しください。私は弊社にて翻訳とコミュニケーションの担当をしている秘書の者です。先月半ばに貴方がこの市にお越しになり、放送の仕事に関する良き提案と指示をして下さったことを存じております。さて、もし差し支えなければ、私が最近書き留め同封いたしました、広島に最初の原子爆弾が投下された際の拙い追憶の記を読んでいただけますでしょうか。貴方が来年4月にアメリカに帰国されると伺いました。先方で日本について書くとき、もしくは話をする時に、この資料を使っていただければ幸いです。いずれにせよ、私は貴方にこの拙い文書を読んでいただけるお時間があり、貴国に持ち帰りいただけるのであればとても喜ばしく思っております。

敬具
尾崎 淳博（おざき あつひろ）

追伸
弊社の児玉氏が貴方にこの手紙と文書を届けてくださいました。

广岛
广岛中央广播电台节目部
1949年3月27日

亲爱的克鲁斯（Crews）先生：

第一次给您写信，请原谅我的冒昧。我是广岛广播电台负责通信和翻译的干事。我知道，上个月中旬，你曾来到广岛，为我们电台的工作提供了宝贵的建议和指导。如果你不介意，请看看我随信附上的笔记。这是我最近写就的有关第一颗原子弹落在广岛的回忆。听说你明年四月份就要回美国。回去后，如果在谈到或写到日本的事情时，你能用到这份材料，我将感到非常荣幸。无论如何，如果你能抽时间看看我的拙作并把它带回你们国家，我将非常高兴。

谨启，
尾崎淳博

另：感谢我们电台热心的儿玉先生将此信和这本笔记带给你。

THE SONG OF

HIROSHIMA

— THE SIXTH OF AUGUST, 1945 —

by

ATSUHIRO OZAKI

Program Section, Hiroshima
Central Broadcasting Station
Hiroshima, Japan

FOREWORD

THE FOURTH MEMORIAL OF THE UNFORGETTABLE DAY, when the first Atom bomb, in the pages of history, fell on the soil and streets of our dear Hiroshima, where the seven rivers with crystal water are still flowing, on August 6, 1945, is coming in a few months. Now it is Spring; the cherry blossoms as before are blooming on the banks, where our beloved ones used to stroll; the larks are still singing in the sky; and from the frozen soil the greens are peeping out again. Flowers on the graves where our beloved ones lay, opened many times and faded away. Nature is unchangeable, but human beings have changed; our once beloved ones are no more and our old homes with cozy rooms and dear furniture are gone! However, God takes and gives. Some of us remain in spite of the trial, having hope and strength to live on.

The new day started at that historical moment. From the destruction and the ashes left by the Atom bomb, the survivors got up for the new day, full of "freedom from fear." From the windows of the newly built, narrow barrack, bright lights are shining on the burned gardens, and the melodies of "the Song of the Reconstruction of Hiroshima" are echoing in the dark starry sky,

> *"Let's reconstruct Hiroshima,*
> *It's daybreak and morning, we are cheerful;*
> *Sounds of hammers are echoing in the morning wind,*
> *Hope arising from the Atom Desert."*

Yes! Reconstruction and hope.

Now, let me explain why I am going to write this note; on the morning of the unforgettable day, I was working at the office of the Hiroshima Central Broadcasting Station, which was located within one kilometer of the center where the first Atom bomb fell. About thirty-five of my co-workers were killed, and my dear mother who was in our home in the suburbs of the city passed away after a serious injury, too. Luckily for me I was safe, not slightly injured, because I was in a room enclosed by a thick wall. What a bitter experience it was to lose my dear mother, my home, my furniture, my favorite books and belongings and also the office where I had worked. Is there such a great event recorded in human history, which resulted in so much loss in one moment?

At that time Hiroshima had about 366,000 inhabitants. By the first Atom bomb 92,133 citizens died by radiation or by being crushed under houses; 9,428 people were seriously wounded, 27,997 were slightly injured, survivals numbered 176,987, and 8,200 houses (90% of the city) were burnt to ashes; the percentage of the dead by radiation increased daily to 70,000 from 46,185. (In these figures the soldiers and service men are not included.) And well-known sites and precious historical monuments and buildings are gone! All gone! And our beloved ones and all things faded away at one moment!

Storm comes after storm; beside this disaster, within about one month, on September 17th, a great flood came to this part of Japan like a ghost and great damage was done. (1,199 persons died or drowned, 897 unknown, and other great damage of houses and rural lands.)

Sometimes in the post-war period, I have talked with my friends in our office, that we should record such a terrible experience and event as materials for the coming generation, though we were poor in writing or could not mention what we intended to do. However, at that time we were very busy setting up new houses, reconstructing our lives and our job at the broadcasting station, and almost four years have passed like a dream. But it is not a dream; it is a fact that there will be no more strife or wars among mankind in the future.

Peace has come to this feudal country where our comrades suffered long under oppressor and dictator! A New Age has indeed come! As for me, what I saw with my eyes and heard with my ears and what I experienced with my whole being on that day, I must write in memo, or diary; it's my duty to our country and to the peace-loving people of the world,

> *"I for Japan,*
> *Japan for the World,*
> *The world for Christ,*
> *And all for God"*
> — Kanzo Uchimura

Indeed this is a human document, intending to mention the vivid events and the true facts, which took place on the morning of the first Atom bomb falling on the city. However I am afraid, by my poor knowledge of English I can't sketch rightly what I experienced, but the narration of the fact itself would prove what happened truly. About scientifically, medical research, someone else must do; my aim is to describe only my personal record of it.

As to my professional career, after being graduated from Kwansei Gakuin, a Methodist Church University, founded by Dr. Lambreth an American missionary, I was once a pastor, an English teacher, a newspaperman, and am now a radio man of the Hiroshima Central Broadcasting Station, living in a humble cottage on the Atom Desert, being an usual civilian, enjoying the daily life of New Japan.

Atsuhiro Ozaki
May 1949

CHAPTER 1

THE DAY

"Christian joy is enhanced by suffering."

— PEAK

IT WAS INDEED THE SIXTH OF AUGUST 1945. Hot and bright days had continued, but by the attacks of the U.S. Planes day by day, and night after night, most important points and cities were crushed or burned to ashes in the latter part of 1944, already Tokyo and its suburbs had received several attacks and terrible damage. America had taken Mariana Isles; and from there B-29s freely attacked our cities and important points. January 3, 1945, 90 planes came to Nagoya; Taiwan and Okinawa were attacked; and bombed by 500 carrier-planes; January 30, U.S. Army and Navy ventured to land at Manila Bay; on the 16th of February U.S. Task Forces landed on Iwo-shima (Island) where the most terrible fights in history were held. On March 13th Osaka and 17th Kobe received much damage and fire respectively. And on the 21st of the same month, Iwo-shima was captured at last by U.S. Task Forces after the loss of many lives and guns on both sides. By this time most of the important cities and bases of these Islands were attacked by B-29s or carrier-planes; and houses and important points burned and destroyed; people loitered about without home, clothes, or food. Where could the lost sheep go? Japan was in the agony of her last day-death.

With these reports and news we were in a melancholy mood and gradually were becoming aware of the coming miserable fortune and dark days. The leaders of the Government tried to make the people believe in the final victory; but they cried out in vain.

Now the day was very hot from the morning. At that time the work which I was in charge of the radio station was that of air-defense communications, receiving the news of the whereabouts of the enemy's planes, from both Military and Naval bases of Hiroshima and Kure, and after writing up hurriedly and roughly the contents I received, I used to hand the scripts to the announcer who was impatiently waiting by my side, to put them on the air. These jobs lasted about two years from morning till night, having no time to rest, and always nervously answering the bells of the telephones.

At two o'clock in that morning an air-raid warning was announced, two or three airplanes were flying over Hiroshima Districts, but about 6 o'clock it was released, though the enemy's planes were still near Hiroshima. This was a misunderstanding of the officers in charge of the base; by the release, the citizens who had run away out of the city the previous night and who had been in the air-raid shelters came home; and were taking breakfast or preparing to go to offices or factories; and some were already on the streets or in the gardens, being refreshed by the morning breezes after fears and fatigues from the previous night. As it is the usual Japanese custom, in the hot summer season, especially men and boys who are staying in doors are naked putting on no clothes or simply putting on Japanese yukata (some simple Summer clothes) or short-pants.

At that very moment, when the clock pointed to nearly 8:15 A.M., the first Atom bomb in history fell on the land of Hiroshima! The centre of it was somewhere near the Aigi-bridge, almost at the centre of the city. Luckily for me, as the telephone from the Military base rang loudly, (it was about 8 A.M.) I dashed into the air-defense communications room with two announcers to receive information, and when I had finished filling up the news blank and handed it to the announcer in charge, I heard a great sound, with the screaming of men for help, and at the same time some crumbs of ceiling fell upon my head; and I saw also some current of blue light something like acetylene light which entered and covered the whole room. I felt that our station had received a direct hit.

Covering my head with a cushion which was on the chair, and trembling with fear of what the world would become, I rushed into the room of the Program Section; Lo! The room had changed! There was no room to step in, because most of the desks and chairs and other pieces of furniture as well as window-glass were broken and fallen; some of my co-workers had fallen on the floor with their faces and bodies injured very much by the bomb-blast. Blood was gushing from their faces and hands; someone was screaming for help, as his eye was cut by a piece of glass caused by the blast. In this calamity I did not know what to do. A certain newspaperman of the Dōmei Tsūshinsha (a well-known Japanese News agency before the War) dashed to me naked and asked me for something to put on. So I gave him a khaki uniform, which happened to be there. As for me I hurried up to my desk and luckily for me I found my cap, my suit, and a rucksack which contained my personal belongings for an urgent occasion.

After a moment, all the workers over there were picking up their clothes and personal things and preparing to run away, in spite of their wounds on head or hands or feet; some already had run away to some safer places. A fire broke out from some comer of the station, but it was put out by the pumps.

I looked out from the broken window, Lo! All the wooden houses in my sight had fallen down or were crushed into pieces and from somewhere smoke and fire already were arising. I wondered what had happened. On the street before the radio station, I saw many citizens who were wounded seriously, almost with naked bodies or only shirts or short pants running to the North of the city in groups or alone. Intimates or friends were helping or carrying by hand the seriously wounded men and women, and children in agony of pain. And from their faces or hands or breasts, I saw blood gushing. Children were calling out the names of their lost parents and brothers in vain. Some were running on the street with not a piece of clothing on their injured bodies. When I saw how the citizens were suffering from the disaster, I recollected some terrible passages and scenes of Dante's Inferno in *Paradise Lost* that I read when I was young.

I recognized that all the city was destroyed, but could not understand why we had such a terrible and miserable result in one moment; it was a mystery; and no one knew the truth at that urgent moment, only coming to the vague conclusion that a powerful, large bomb had fallen on the ground or some special electrical power had prevailed upon the city and the suburbs by some scientific means.

In this calamity, however, I came to myself, and contrived some way to get from this dangerous place to another safer shelter. I first thought of my sick mother and of my only son in the factory, but fire had already broken out in that part of the city and I could not return there. God may protect them! So through the Sakae-bridge, which is nearest to our station, I intended to go to "the Eastern Drill Ground." As my decision was settled, I hurriedly prepared to put on my suit and the rucksack. And on my way down to the first floor I discovered a girl announcer, Miss Izawa, lying on the floor, who could not walk after receiving a bruise on the foot. With my friends I carried her to the gate, where I found Mr. Majima, sub-chief of the Program Section, lying with bloody body, calling for help; some were there surrounding him.

At that time a certain girl held my hand and requested me to save her father who was crushed under the timbers and could not move, while several friends were calling out to be saved. And a child about two years old was crying out, seeking her lost mother near the Gate. I was at a loss what I should do. But I made up my minds to help first the girl announcer and our chief; so with the help of my friends I put a board on a baby carriage which fortunately I found near the gate, and upon it we let them lay. But they were too heavy and it crushed immediately, causing the two wounded ones to fall on the ground. So as to the chief, I put him under the care of my friends, while I determined to carry the girl on my shoulder. But she was so heavy and the heat of the summer sun was so severe that it was very difficult to carry her on my shoulder; besides these, the road was full of fallen timbers and poles and spreading breakstones.

Carrying the girl, I walked about two blocks, after stumbling and falling on the ground two or three times because she was so heavy. At this time few people were running away and from several places near-by a fire arose. We stopped before the gate of a great mansion owned by Mr. Awaya, the chief Administrator of the Chugoku District. I discovered the walls of it were very thick and strong; and also beside the gate there was a rain-water tank. I reckoned that this would be the safest place for her for a while, saying "Miss Izawa! I guess this is a safe place; there are wall and a water-tank. You better wait until I shall find a vehicle to carry you." She nodded. Though it seemed to be cruel to say this to Miss Izawa, I could not help saying so, because danger was surrounding us.

After I parted with her, I was told afterwards, as she was surrounded with fire, she jumped into the water-tank with an old woman who happened to pass by and they spent the night in the tank uneasily and next day she was found and was saved by the rescue car of the Hiroshima Communication Bureau's Hospital and was carried to the hospital and was healed, while her father died on that day and also her mother was wounded. But now she has recovered and is working as a clerk in a certain Printing Co., in Hiroshima and living with her mother. On the first Memorial Day of the Atom bomb falling, she called on me and thanked me with a bundle of rice. What a happy meeting it was!

After I parted with the girl, I began to run in the direction of the Bridge. On my way there I found again Mr. Majima our chief, lying on the road and by him I found his wife there, crying out to me, "Mr. Ozaki! Come and help my husband!" Luckily I saw Mr. Date (who afterwards died) running along the road. I called and requested him to help our chief; as he consented I brought a board from a near-by broken house and put our chief on it, and we began to carry him. After we walked about one block, we found a crushed house with a broad garden. We thought this would be a safe shelter for a moment, so we entered the gate and put him down in one corner of the garden. By this time fire had come from two directions; so with Mr. Date, we said good-by to our chief and his wife.

What happened to Mr. Majima afterwards? When I went to the spot where we parted with him after two days, I did not find him or his remains; maybe some rescue party had carried him to bury him in some place. As to his wife, she afterwards explained to me that after we parted with them her husband passed away within five minutes; Lo she ran with the daughter of the chief-administrator who happened to pass by, to the river and then to the police station and there she went to the East Drill Ground, and after passing uneasily two nights over there, she went to her intimate friend's home west of the city. She is a daughter of Mr. Iwao Kongo, a well-known Japanese classic musician, "Noh Song" singer.

After I parted with my chief and his wife, with much difficulty, I came to the Bridge, but I could not cross it, because all the houses beyond the bridge were burning. And from behind me fire broke out too, so I jumped down upon the sands from the bank of the River. My rucksack, which I was holding in my hand, fell into the water; it floated! At first I thought I would give up trying to get it. But the contents of it was everything I had in this wide, wide world; bank notes, some clothes, some food, and other important belongings it contained; Therefore I changed my mind and jumped into the water, caught the floating bag after swimming about three minutes.

I sat down on the sands and thought what I should do and no good ideas or plans came into my mind. Under the bridge I found about 200 refugees clustered on the sands. Most of them were wearing torn bloody clothes and were seriously injured; especially their faces, and also they were barefooted and had no belongings or bags. Then a group of Military men (about five in all) came holding a regimental flag. A certain lieutenant among them had his hand wounded and it was bleeding; he asked me to bind his hand; as I had not a piece of cloth to bind it, I tore a piece of my white shirt and bound the bloody hand. He thanked me very much. After a while, these soldiers found a little boat and holding the flag they rowed up the river. The fire beyond the bridge was fanned by a strong wind and pieces of timbers blew to this part of the river; as it was very dangerous, we jumped frequently into the water to get out of it. By this time I felt very hungry because I had not taken breakfast that morning. I found a piece of onion floating on the water; I caught it after swimming and ate it with some raw rice that I had found in my rucksack. I discovered, in an urgent time any poor thing to eat could satisfy the stomach.

About 10 o'clock in the morning, rains with dark clouds began to fall upon the faces of the miserable refugees. At this time I heard some great sounds of bombing continually. People on that spot feared they might be some attacks from planes; and they ran about on the narrow place here and there, but soon they were informed that they were the explosions of a certain powder magazine. By this time fire was in every direction. I felt very lonely thinking my end was coming. But luckily for me the water of the River was gradually going down and the surface of more sands appeared. Over there a quarter of a mile away, I knew that there was "The East Police Station" and I had intended to go to the station to receive instant help; so I began to walk down on the sands along the bank.

CHAPTER 2

OVER THE HILLS

"When a door closes, a window opens."

—ITALIAN PROVERB

I WALKED ON THE SANDS; SOMETIMES JUMPED ON THEM. Fire in every part of the city lasted the rest of day; glaring heat and smoke covered the whole sky and land. I heard the sounds of cracking of the falling houses caused by fire: tall trees were burning and breaking up in the sky, sparking like electric currents. I saw the hill beyond the city smoking. The summer sun cruelly shone upon the heads of the miserable people. I saw on the sands of the river many refugees, wounded and depressed in spirit, intimates and friends helping them, binding the wounded with some pieces of cloth. A baby in the hands of its mother passing away; their countenances expecting coming troubles were covered with miserable and hopeless moods. Where would they go? Where could the lost aunts, brothers and sisters and beloved ones be now? How would food for the coming day and night be supplied?

"I am not at ease, neither am I quiet, neither have I rest; but trouble cometh."

With Job I could not help complaining.

I climbed upon the bank from the sands of the River. Here and there I saw a great many dead; men and women, old and young, children and babies as well as dogs and cats; some with half of their faces burned; some cut by pieces of glass and being naked, and blackened by smoke and fire. I could not bear to see these miserable shapes. The smell of the dead mixed with the smoke of burning houses prevailed in the air and on the streets.

I stood on the high place of the bank and looked around. Fire after fire; crush after crush. Hiroshima, our dear city is burning! Our dear abode is coming to the very end. All gone. No more Hiroshima; Fire in the east and fire in the west. And from every direction. It's very hot. The citizens had died and were buried; houses falling, tramcars and motorcars burning! West of where I stood, I saw cruel flares of fire current pushing out from the windows of the tall concrete Chugoku Press Building and the giant Fukuya Department Store. The cross of the longer tower of the Methodist Church where I used to go on Sundays was smoking. Only the concrete buildings kept their shape or structure, though the furniture and other things in doors were burned ashes. I knew our radio station would remain in spite of the burning of he inner part, as it was a concrete one.

At last I came to the East Station, but there were no offices on duty; several wounded policemen were lying in the room. In a comer I found fresh water gushing out from a broken supply. I drank. It was so sweet after thirst by heat and the summer sun, that I drank several cups of it. Near the office there were several bicycles that were going to bum. I made up my mind to borrow a bicycle without permission at this urgent time because there were none to ask about it. God would pardon me! I did need it to get away from the fire and the danger. So picking up one I rode on to the eastern part of the city, through the burning streets and crossing smoking bridges many times.

After much difficulty, at last I came to the Eastern Drill Ground, where I found here and there a group of refugees resting on the dry ground, all fatigued after the trial, being wounded, and almost naked and having no personal belongings with them. People were carrying some seriously wounded persons on boards or on their shoulders.

I lay down on the grass, and looking up into the sky, I breathed deeply the fresh air. It was so fresh as I had been breathing the smoky air in the burning city. I felt I was very tired and was thinking what to do now? I remembered I had been told that if our broadcasting station (the studio) was destroyed on a tragic occasion, we would remove and gather at the Hara Broadcast-ing Station, which was located about two miles northward from our studio. But the direct way there through Yokoyawa Street had been closed by fire; so I decided to reach the destination at first by going around the east side of the Hara Village from here and then passing over the hill and crossing the River, I would reach the station in Hara.

As I decided to do so, I felt some hope arising in my heart. This place where I lay down was in the eastern suburbs of Hiroshima. Though the houses near-by were far away from the city, some burned or all the roofs, window-glass and some weak parts of them were blasted, some houses were half fallen by the strong blast... Wounded people were loitering here and there crying for help. There were few people who had not received wounds, I thanked God that I was safe.

And after thirty minutes' rest, I started again to ride on the way to the hill. It was about two o'clock. I felt I was hungry. When I was riding on I happened to see a certain house by the road. Abruptly I went into the gate without knowing who lived in it; a middle aged woman and a girl were there. There were also many refugees in every room. I explained to them how I had run away from the burning city and wanted to rest for a while; they led me in a room and served me kindly with cakes and tea. As I had some rice in my rucksack, I cooked it myself with potatoes that the woman gave me. After finishing lunch I said good-by to them and rode upon the hill again. On my way I saw lots of Navy trucks carrying many wounded people and dashing on the road of the hill to the northward. The refugees were almost naked, their faces and hair were burned, and some were wearing bloody clothes, so I could not recognize whether they were male or female.

Slowly a car came after me; I glanced in the car and saw a noble Military officer lying with his wounded face bound up; afterwards I was told that he was a Korean prince who was in the service of the Army; and he had received a serious wound near the Aioi Bridge, the centre of the atom falling on that day, when he was riding a horse, while his adjutant feeling his responsibili-ties that he was not near his master, committed suicide. On my way there was a primary school. Many refugees gathered there and the wounded were receiving medical treatments and being served with handouts of biscuits or rice.

At this time the hill becoming steeper, I got down from my bicycle and began to walk. A truck filled with the wounded dashed on; when a woman's voice was heard from the truck calling my name,

"Mr. Ozaki! Mr. Ozaki!"

"Who are you?" I wondered.

"I am Yamazaki, an official girl of the Radio Station. I received a serious wound on my back," she said.

She was sitting in the middle of the car wearing two simple pieces and having a sad countenance.

"Oh you were! Be careful of yourself. God will help you! About you I am sure to tell the manager. Please wait a bit."

The truck passed by and disappeared. As for her, she recovered after receiving medical treatment and is now working in our station.

I met two office girls of our station on the way and one was walking with a stick as her foot was injured. I asked how they had run this way from the station; from it they had run to the River, after they crossed it in a boat just floating near they came this way crossing over the hill of Ushida. I congratulated them. And I parted with them, as they were going to their friend's home near the village.

After one hour or so I came to the River and I had to cross it. There was a ferryboat, being rowed by a boy. He kindly took me and my bicycle on that boat. After I landed at the other side of the river, I requested him to tell me the fare.

"The fare? Did you think I can request money from the refugee? You have come from Hiroshima, I guess; from a refugee can I request money? Rather I must help you."

I was moved very much and I felt my eyes moisten. He knew how his comrades of this country were suffering from the disaster!

I came upon the bank. It was twilight. I asked some villager the way to the Hara Broad-casting Station and I was told I was in a twenty-minute ride of it. A truck was dashing in the direction of Hiroshima, loaded with foods and rations; when it passed by me, some one in the truck threw something to me, I found it was some biscuits and I thanked them, as a heavenly gift. And six-thirty in the evening, safely I arrived at the station. There were already about ten of my co-workers who had reached there from the city and were waiting for the rest of the workers to arrive. They were quite at a loss by the big event. The manager was there, and I explained to him all my experience in detail. The friends of the station welcomed me and gave me a towel and other things and served me a dish of warm rice and soup.

I discovered, though this station is about three miles away from Hiroshima, it had also received some damage by the Atom bomb, having the window-glass or the roofs of the office broken by the blast, and I understood how big the effect of the Atom bomb was. The station has a broad garden around the office. I went out in the garden; in the darkness I saw the flowers of bush-clover already beginning to bloom here and there in the garden. It was still, but on the southern sky about three miles beyond, I saw a great fire was still burning over the city fiercely and as brightly as daytime.

It is Hiroshima! Our dearest city, our abode! I knelt down on the grass and prayed to God for the safety of mother, who was in our home, and my only son, named Sei-ichi, who was working in some factory near the city, and my friends and their families who were not yet discovered by that time. Is this the end of Hiroshima? And the end of my life? I prayed; I felt God was helping me; in spite of calamity or misfortune God was still near me; there were some rooms to live in; some shelter to live in at some corner in this part of Japan. Disaster strengthened me. I remembered some verses from the Scripture —

"But we glory in tribulations also; knowing that tribulations worketh patience; and patience, experience; and experience, hope—"

Yes! Experience and hope! Cold wind awoke me from my meditations; I went in and prepared to sleep in the blankets on the hard floor. But I could not sleep a bit, and passed the night uneasy in mind and body.

CHAPTER 3

SEEKING AFTER MY BELOVED ONES

"Obviously, circumstances alone do not make us happy or unhappy. Our feelings are determined by the way we react to them. We can all endure disaster and triumph over it — if we have to. — We are stronger than we think."

— DALE CARNEGIE

GOT UP WITH DROWSY EYES. I FELT DULL IN MY BODY. Men in ordinary times can manage the right way, but on urgent occasion, it is difficult to do the right way as occasion may require; and when people are at a loss facing disaster, they can't react against disaster. With the cold wind of the morning we came to ourselves, and the thought of the first step that we had to carry on, came across our minds. So the first step we had to do in the morning was to let our Tokyo Radio Station know our urgent event. The most of the trunk lines and other sending lines were cut by the blast; however we discovered there remained a line between Hiroshima and Tokyo through Himeji City. So we sent a short report, saying "the city was destroyed by the attack of the planes, our station received fire, many deaths of workers, great fatal damage etc." There were lots of things to do about our station. But as I have mentioned before, all the sending lines and trunk line were destroyed, we decided, for the next step, to seek after the lost workers and families, while we were waiting help from neighbors' stations and Tokyo.

Therefore I left the station and began to ride on my bicycle to Hiroshima in order to seek after my family. The road to Hiroshima was so crowded with people, coming down and going to the city; wounded people, men carrying heavy rucksacks; cars, carriages and trucks jammed with refugees and things; some excited by the event, some drooping with fatigues and severe heat of summer, that it was very hard to ride. I came to Yokogawa, the entrance of the city. There was a truck full of food and rations; some one called me and gave me a handout of rice. From here it became more difficult to ride on, because many electric poles, fallen houses and lots of timbers and break-stones, stood on the way, the bridges were fallen and burnt. So I could not go to my home directly along the usual way. I had to go around the way, changing my course many times, sometimes crossing the smoking bridge; I stumbled frequently, but by all means, I had to go to the West-bridge, near my home. I saw on the streets and in the rivers a great many corpses. On my way, near the West Telephoning Station, I heard very faint voices from an air raid shelter; I looked into it, and I discovered several naked girls wounded seriously and all their skin burnt, embracing each other; most of them seemed about to die already through moving somehow. I heard a girl with very weak voice, calling "Mother! Mother! " I asked her name but no reply. I could not extend help to them because there were no means to save them. Therefore I closed my eyes and prayed for them. Near by a certain woman, with a baby in her hands, was walking, full of tears. I understand the baby had already passed away.

At last I came to my home, near the Bridge and discovered it burnt to ashes. This was my worst experience in my life. I began to put away ashes and some breakstones and other metals, being afraid that somewhere under them the remains of mother would be found, when I heard a voice behind me—

"Grand-ma is safe."

I was very much surprised to hear it. It was my son, safe and sound. We embraced each other in tears and thanked God. He explained as follows; when he had heard the sound of the bomb at the factory, he was knocked down by the blast, but not injured. He had run home in haste, which was within twenty minutes of the factory; when he had reached home, our home was burning and grand-ma was standing at the gate with neighbors. He had found a carriage, then on it he put grand-ma and the neighbors and began to run away to the nearest village crossing the Bridge. He pulled on about twenty minutes or so, when a reserve truck happened to come and carried them to Jigogen fishing town about six miles away from the city. And they are now staying in a primary school.

I was very glad to hear my son's report; and I immediately made up my mind to go there and see my mother. It was nearly evening when I reached Jigogen town on foot. The barracks of the school were jammed with the refugees. I found my mother resting on a mat at the comer of the ground, somehow excited and wounded in her left foot. She was very glad that I was safe.

Rice and soup were served for us, and clothes and shirts were donated to us. As the rooms of the school were crowded and some of the people were dying, we decided to pass the night on the ground. But by the excitement of the event and stings of mosquitoes we could not sleep well.

CHAPTER 4

THE BURNT CITY

"By suffering men learn."

— BLAISE PASCAL

THE 8TH DAY OF AUGUST CAME WITH SHINING MORNING SUN. I put my mother and son under the care of the officers in charge, saying good-by to them, because I had many, many things to do at the station.

I came to the centre of the city. Lo! It was a desert! People were now calling it the Atom-desert, without inhabitants or trees, indeed no living ones; all the tramcars had stopped, being burnt here and there. The smell of the dead prevailed in the streets and in the air. The strong iron-concrete Aioi Bridge, near the centre of the Atom bomb, was broken in some parts; the thick iron metal being bent and the wall of the bridge being blasted. I had heard about 200 workers of the Hiroshima Post Office were buried and died instantly on the spot, only two or three being saved; and about 600 officers of the Prefectural Government had the same fortune, too. All the passengers in a tramcar that happened to run near the centre, died at one moment on that day! Indeed great sacrifice of humans and things in history.

I came in front of the Fukuya Department Store; gayish lights and cheerful chatterings of sales girls were no more; smoking and burning only the outside concrete walls and floor remained. I came to the cross where there was the Kangyo Bank and there lots of seriously wounded citizens were lying on the floor of the bank. Most of them having the skin of their faces burned; all screaming and crying. Some physicians and nurses were helping them, binding the wounded spots or giving injections.

At last I came to our radio station. The new wooden office on the background was no more, but the main building was there. I entered it from the front gate; all the broadcasting machines and cabinets were broken, and the furniture, books, records, all gone to ashes. Water was gushing out caused by cutting of pipes of water supply and filled the room. I entered our room of Program Section; all changed into ashes except the metals; the room seemed to become broader than ever. I happened to find a mess-tin, which I used to have before the Fire, and I took it for a memorial. And next I went into the air-raid shelter; and found all the important things, personal and official, burnt or filled with water. I climbed up to the top-roof of the station and looked around. It was a desert, nothing remained except some concrete building or half-burnt trees. The Hijiyama Hill was very near, it seemed.

On my way to the Hara Station, I went to see the Old Castle where the Military base was. There was no more castle or military barracks. I found many soldiers' corpses lying in the drill ground and in the ponds around the old castle. The remains and stones of the castle or half-burnt trees only show the dreams of soldiers' past brilliant days. Militarism and feudalism were gone. I loitered for a while on the burnt grass and was recollecting on past days.

In the evening I returned to Hara Station. And we decided to borrow some farmer's room near the station for our workers. Though about thirty-five workers of our station died, it was fortunate all the secretaries of the Program Section were safe. Only some of them had received slight wounds and lost their wives or children

About the great bomb, which fell on Hiroshima, there were lots of rumors, as I have mentioned before. G.H.Q. of Japan announced simply saying a great powerful scientific bomb fell on Hiroshima city effecting great damage of persons and houses. Later we were told, by the information from U.S.A. it was the very Atom bomb that caused the big disaster, and we also understood for the first time that most of the dead or wounded were caused by radiation.

Rumors had spread that no living thing, human or trees could live for seventy-five years in Hiroshima or the suburbs. So the refugees who remained in the broken houses or the air-raid shelter in the city began to remove to other parts of this country. To tell the truth, the percentage of the deaths increased; the citizens who had received radiation felt their hair began to drop out and some specks on the skin appeared; and they died day by day. Some died from infection resulting from the *radiation* of blood. Because all the crematoriums were destroyed, bereaved families of the city had to burn their dead beloved ones by themselves.

In a few days after the event of Hiroshima, the greatest events in the world were the second atom bomb fell at Nagasaki, and the Russian Declaration of war against Japan, as the Russian Army began to attack and invade the borderlines of Manchuria. Misfortune comes after misfortune. How could we sustain such a great attack? The last day of Japan was coming. The Military and the Navy had no power over Japan and the Japanese.

About this time, we are informed that Japan was negotiating peace with the Allied Forces. And later we were told that at noon sharp on August 15, some grave message would be announced by the Emperor, bidding that at that hour all the vehicles and cars should be stopped and hear the message. We were very busy to put this bulletin on the air. People in our country had waited impatiently and anxiously for this moment.

On that day, all the vehicles and men on the streets stopped and people in homes and offices listened eagerly to the radio. At first an announcer from Tokyo was introduced and we heard the voice of our Emperor and knew the last day of the War had come! But un-conditional surrender! I can't express the impression at that historical moment with a pen; how we felt and what would happen in this land afterwards. All wept; wept with mixed feelings respectively. All the service men were released and began to return from abroad. People who during the War, went to villages from cities, prepared to return to their homes or the burnt cities; all the rail-ways or ships or cars were jammed with these people; all taking large rucksacks with them. There was disorder in the cars and in the streets for some period, until the Allied Forces arrived at this shore.

To tell of my personal matter my mother who had returned to the city again and stayed in a half broken house died in the early morning of September 1st because of the serious wound of her foot. I put fuel upon her body to set fire with my son! It seemed to be cruel to do so, but I could not help doing so, on that urgent occasion. God knows. In order to bury her remains,

I was preparing to go to my native country, Shikoku, over the Inland Sea, when a great flood came on September 17 midnight. Rains had lasted several days; at midnight I was awakened by the crying of someone "Flood! Flood!" I opened the window; Lo! The water was coming up to the second floor of the cottage where we were staying. If the house moved by the current of water, what would happen? I saw on the cruel water, many logs and broken houses. We had no means to escape and so we only were waiting the decrease of water and the coming of daybreak. Luckily for us the water began to lower gradually with the coming of morning.

And by day breaking we felt we were safe; water dropped to about two feet. Flood after fire! By this damage of flood, collection of crops and vegetables would be decreased, it was announced. Our hearts were darkened.

As I had mother's remains with me, on that after-noon in the flood, I ventured with my son to go to the harbor that is about four miles south. And after much difficulty, crossing the currents of flood many times. It was night when we came to the city; it was dark and a death-city without inhabitants; we found a broken tramcar and stayed in it about two hours for rest, and started again to the harbor. Early the next morning we took a boat for my native country to bury the remains of my mother.

One day on a bright autumn day of the year, soldiers of the Occupied Forces arrived at Kure, ex-naval port. The new day had come!

CHAPTER 5

THE PEACE HAS COME

"We do not intend that the Japanese shall be enslaved as a race or destroyed as a Nation…. The Japanese Government shall remove all obstacles to the revivals and strengthening of Democratic tendencies among the Japanese people."

— FROM POTSDAM DECLARATION

FOUR YEARS HAVE PASSED SINCE THE UNFORGETTABLE DAY when the first Atom bomb fell on the land of Hiroshima. Now Japan where there is no more war has started its first step as a nation of Democracy. All has changed! Feudalistic Japan has gone! The New Constitution of Japan was declared on November 3, 1947. And "freedom of speech, of religion, and of thought, as well as respect for the fundamental human rights" was established. Service men were released. All the soldiers abroad, from China, Siberia, and the South Seas have returned to their burnt and broken native places. Military and Navy were completely disarmed, while Japanese Sovereignty was limited to the old islands, losing many of her colonies. In consequence, the population of the post-war of this country would become 80,000,000 people in the near future in this small area. On the other hand, the political and social conditions were in disorder for a while With the inflation, daily living is becoming harder day by day; black-markets increased every where. Houses, food and clothes were few and the prices of them were becoming higher daily. Thieves, burglars, and murderers filled the cells of the police stations. Uneasy days and restless nights have lasted long. Especially young folks who had received military education and training seemed to have lost their aim in life. And they also misunderstood the true meaning of Democracy; their way of life has become rough and disorderly, loitering in the streets or in the black-markets, or committing burglary in groups.

On bookstands, cheap, immoral books, magazines, and printed matter are selling. While housewives had to go to the farms to buy rice, corn and vegetables from the farmer, exchanging for them their essential dresses.

Indeed Japan was in a crucible of disorder. But from the latter part of the third year, social conditions have become better in some degree; Allied Forces, especially U.S.A. and English, have extended their hands very much, food, clothes and other things were sent to this shore; Unrra [United Nations Relief and Rehabilitation Administration] and Lara [Licensed Agencies for Relief in Asia] goods are enlivening the orphans or widows or homeless folks; foods have increased, clothes were supplied, houses have been built.

Hope and reconstruction! We must carry on our new plans for them in spite of the disasters. In Hiroshima, at present we have 245,000 inhabitants (before the atom 312,200) and houses 60,000 (before the day 76,000) Department-Stores, banks, cinema-shows and the official and private publications have started their jobs; the tram-cars began to run; warm tea-rooms and nice cafes and restaurants have opened their doors.

Ships full of cargo from abroad are in the harbor of Ujina; and foreigners are visiting daily to see the ruins of the Atom City, wondering how great the influence of the Atom bomb. Hiroshima is reviving. The campaign of "no more Hiroshimas" is now active in the world as well as in Japan.

Now we are echoing with joy and hope that "the Japanese people forever renounce war as a sovereign right of the nation and the threat or use of force as a means of settling international disputes," as the new Constitution of Japan declares to the peace-loving people. So it is not the last day of Hiroshima, but the first, hopeful day of it.

— THE END —

LA CANCIÓN DE

HIROSHIMA

Traducción al español
Andrés Rosende

PREFACIO

por

NOEL CAPON

EN 1999, LOIS CREWS MURIÓ A LOS 94 AÑOS EN PORT WASHINGTON, LONG ISLAND, NUEVA YORK. Como mi mujer y yo éramos los parientes más cercanos de Lois y su casa iba aser vendida, Deanna y yo nos encargamos de revisar y organizar sus pertenencias, y dedecidir qué guardar y qué subastar. Buscando en el ático, encontré un escrito en un cuaderno infantil. Unas semanas más tarde leí el cuaderno y ahora Wessex publica *La canción de Hiroshima*.

Antes de la Segunda Guerra Mundial, el marido de Lois, Albert Crews, trabajaba para la NBC. Después de la guerra, y bajo las órdenes del General MacArthur, pasó varias semanas en Hiroshima instruyendo al personal de la emisora de radio. Albert recibió el manuscrito de Atsuhiro Ozaki, el encargado de las comunicaciones y traducciones de la emisora.

El 6 de agosto de 1945, el señor Ozaki trabajaba en la emisora de radio, a menos de un kilómetro de donde cayó la bomba. El cuaderno que entregó a Albert Crews relata lo que hizo y vio durante los tres días siguientes a la explosión. Al entregarle el manuscrito a Albert Crews, el señor Ozaki quiso compartir sus experiencias con la gente de Estados Unidos. No sabemos si Albert llegó a utilizar este material o si el cuaderno pasó medio siglo sentado en el ático de Port Washington. Sea como fuere, y a pesar de que han pasado ya 60 años, esta publicación hace realidad los deseos de Atsuhiro Ozaki.

Con la intención de conceder a este material una amplia distribución, Wessex publica *La canción de Hiroshima* en inglés, japonés, español y chino. También reproducimos la carta que Atsuhiro Ozaki escribió a Albert Crews e incluimos el manuscrito original en su totalidad. Esta publicación incluye pequeñas correcciones ortográficas y editoriales del texto original para facilitar su comprensión.

Noel Capon
Bronxville, Nueva York
1 de enero, 2011

Noel Capon es el profesor R.C. Kopf de Marketing Internacional en la Escuela de Negocios de la Universidad de Columbia, Nueva York. Deanna Kuhn es profesora de Psicología y Educación en el Teachers College de la Universidad de Columbia, Nueva York.

LA CANCIÓN DE

HIROSHIMA

— SEIS DE AGOSTO DE 1945 —

por

ATSUHIRO OZAKI

Sección de programación, Hiroshima
Centro de emisiones
Hiroshima, Japón

PRÓLOGO

"Una época sin gran angustia en el corazón, no tiene gran música en su vida."

— KARL BARTH

FALTAN POCOS MESES PARA EL CUARTO ANIVERSARIO DEL DÍA INOLVIDABLE, cuando la primera bomba atómica en las páginas de la historia cayó sobre la tierra y calles de nuestra querida Hiroshima, donde los siete ríos de aguas cristalinas siguen corriendo, el 6 de agosto de 1945. Ahora es primavera, y los cerezos florecen, como antes, en las orillas por las que nuestros seres queridos solían pasear; las alondras todavía cantan en el cielo; y de la tierra helada empiezan de nuevo a salir brotes verdes. Las flores en las tumbas donde yacen nuestros seres queridos han florecido y se han marchitado muchas veces. La naturaleza no cambia, pero los seres humanos han cambiado; nuestros seres queridos han fallecido y nuestras viejas casas con sus acogedoras habitaciones y queridos muebles han desaparecido. Sin embargo, Dios nos da y Dios nos quita. Algunos de nosotros todavía seguimos aquí, a pesar de las duras pruebas, teniendo esperanza y fuerza para seguir adelante.

El nuevo día comenzó en un momento histórico. De la destrucción y de las cenizas que dejó la bomba atómica, los supervivientes despertaron a un nuevo día "libres de miedo". Desde las ventanas de los estrechos barracones, intensas luces brillan sobre los jardines quemados y las melodías de la "canción de la reconstrucción de Hiroshima" resuenan en el oscuro cielo estrellado,

> *"Reconstruyamos Hiroshima,*
> *El día rompe en la mañana, estamos alegres;*
> *El sonido de los martillos resuena en el viento de la mañana,*
> *La esperanza nace del desierto atómico."*

¡Si! Reconstrucción y esperanza.

Ahora, déjenme explicar por qué escribo estas notas; en la mañana del día inolvidable, trabajaba en la oficina de la Estación Central de Emisiones de Hiroshima, situada a menos de un kilómetro del epicentro donde la primera bomba atómica cayó. Treinta y cinco de mis compañeros de trabajo perecieron, y mi querida madre, que estaba en su casa en los suburbios de la ciudad, murió también de graves heridas. Afortunadamente, yo salí ileso, sin ni siquiera un rasguño, porque me encontraba en una habitación rodeada por un grueso muro. ¡Qué experiencia más amarga fue perder a mi madre, mi casa, mis muebles, mis libros preferidos y todas mis pertenencias, y también la oficina en la que había trabajado! ¿Existe algún otro acontecimiento en la historia de la humanidad en el que tanto se perdió en tan sólo un momento?

En aquel entonces, Hiroshima tenías 366.000 habitantes. Después de la bomba, 92.133 ciudadanos perdieron la vida a causa de las radiaciones o aplastados bajo sus casas; 9.428 resultaron gravemente heridos y 22.997 heridos leves, siendo 176.987 el número total de supervivientes. 8.200 casas (el 90% de la ciudad) se convirtió en cenizas. El porcentaje de muertos a causa de las radiaciones aumentaba diariamente hasta alcanzar los 70.000. (Estas cifras no incluyen a los soldados y hombres de servicio). Y conocidas localizaciones e históricos monumentos y edificios desaparecieron. ¡Todo desapareció! ¡Y nuestros seres queridos y todas las cosas se desvanecieron en un instante!

Una tormenta sigue a otra; un mes después del desastre, el 17 de septiembre, una gran inundación azotó esta parte de Japón, causando grandes daños (1.199 personas murieron o se ahogaron, 897 desaparecieron y otros graves daños materiales se infligieron a casas y terrenos rurales.)

A veces, en la época de postguerra, comentaba con mis compañeros de oficina que deberíamos documentar estas experiencias y eventos terribles como material de aprendizaje para las siguientes generaciones, a pesar de que ninguno escribía demasiado bien y no teníamos una idea clara de cómo hacerlo. En aquel tiempo estábamos muy ocupados levantando nuevas casas, reconstruyendo nuestras vidas y con nuestros trabajos en la emisora, y casi cuatro años pasaron como un sueño. Pero no es un sueño; es un hecho que no habrá más conflictos ni guerras entre hombres en el futuro.

La paz ha llegado a este país feudal donde nuestros camaradas han sufrido durante mucho tiempo bajo el mando del opresor y dictador. ¡Una Nueva Era ha llegado! Y en cuanto a mi, lo que vi con mis ojos y escuché con mis oídos y la experiencia que sufrí con todo mi ser aquel día, debo escribirla; es mi deber con mi país y con la gente que ama la paz en todo el mundo,

> *"Yo, por Japón,*
> *Japón por el mundo,*
> *El mundo por Cristo,*
> *Y todos por Dios"*
> — Kanzo Uchimura

Esto es, efectivamente, un documento humano, que escribo con la intención de recordar los eventos y los hechos que tuvieron lugar la mañana del primer día en el que la primera bomba atómica cayó en la ciudad. Sin embargo, me temo que por mi pobre conocimiento del inglés, no pueda esbozar con claridad toda mi experiencia, aunque la narración de los hechos mismos demuestre que fue verdad lo que pasó. Mi intención aquí es tan solo describir mi experiencia personal. La investigación científica y médica la dejo para otros.

En cuanto a mi carrera profesional, después de licenciarme en Kwansei Gakuin, una universidad de la Iglesia Metodista fundada por el Dr. Lambreth, un misionero americano, fui pastor, profesor de inglés, periodista y, ahora, un hombre de radio en la Estación de Emisiones Central de Hiroshima. Vivo en una humilde cabaña en el desierto atómico, siendo un civil más y disfrutando de la vida diaria del Nuevo Japón.

Atsuhiro Ozaki
Mayo 1949

CAPÍTULO 1

EL DÍA

"La alegría cristiana aumenta con el sufrimiento."

— PEAK

ERA, EFECTIVAMENTE, EL SEIS DE AGOSTO DE 1945. Los días eran cálidos y soleados. Debido a los constantes ataques de los aviones estadounidenses, día tras día, noche tras noche, las ciudades y puntos más importantes habían sido aplastados o reducidas a cenizas a finales de 1944, e incluso Tokio y alrededores habían recibido varios ataques y daños terribles. Estados Unidos había tomado las islas Mariana y desde allí mandaba a sus B-29 a atacar frecuentemente nuestras ciudades. El 3 de enero de 1945, noventa aviones atacaron Nagoya y quinientos Taiwan y Okinawa; el 30 de enero, la armada y marina americana desembarcaron en la Bahía de Manila; el 16 de febrero las fuerzas especiales estadounidenses llegaron a la isla de Iwo-shima donde tendría lugar la más terrible de las batallas. El 13 de marzo Osaka y el 17 Kobe son fuertemente atacadas y dañadas. Y el 21 del mismo mes, las fuerzas especiales capturan Iwo-shima con fuertes pérdidas humanas en ambos bandos. En este momento la mayoría de las ciudades y bases de las islas han sido atacadas por aviones B-29; las casas y los puntos de importancia han sido destruidos; la gente deambula sin casa, ropa o comida. ¿Donde se habría metido la oveja perdida? Japón agonizaba esperando el día de su muerte.

Con estos informes y noticias, nos encontrábamos sumidos en la melancolía y, poco a poco, nos dábamos cuenta de la miserable fortuna y los días oscuros que se nos venían encima. Y, mientras tanto, los líderes del gobierno intentaban, en vano, convencer a la gente de que la victoria final era posible.

Los días eran muy calurosos desde la mañana. Mi trabajo en la emisora de radio consistía en controlar las comunicaciones de defensa aérea. Recibía noticias sobre el paradero de aviones enemigos desde las bases militares y navales de Hiroshima y Kure y, tras una apresurada redacción, las pasaba al locutor para su emisión. Este trabajo duró dos años enteros, desde la mañana hasta la noche, sin tiempo para descansar y siempre nervioso cuando sonaban los teléfonos.

A las dos de la mañana de ese día, se dio la alerta de una redada aérea. Dos o tres aviones volaban sobre distritos de Hiroshima. Sobre las seis de la mañana la alerta cesó, a pesar de que los aviones enemigos seguían cerca de Hiroshima. Fue un malentendido de los oficiales al mando de la base pues, al cesar la alerta, todas aquellas personas que habían huido de la ciudad y que se encontraban en los refugios antiaéreos, regresaron a casa; y se encontraban desayunando o preparándose para ir a las fábricas o a las oficinas; otros ya estaban en las calles o en los jardines, refrescándose con la brisa de mañana, después del miedo y la fatiga de la noche anterior. Como es habitual en Japón durante el caluroso verano, los hombre y niños que estaban en el interior de sus casas andaban sin ropa, o simplemente con pantalones cortos o una *yukata* (rompas simples de verano).

En aquél preciso momento, cuando el reloj señalaba casi las 8:15 AM, la primera bomba atómica de la historia cayó sobre Hiroshima. El epicentro de la explosión fue cerca del puente de Aigi, casi el centro de la ciudad. Afortunadamente para mi, y mientras el teléfono de la base militar sonaba con fuerza (eran como las 8:00 AM), me encontraba en la sala de comunicaciones de defensa aérea con otras dos personas. Cuando terminé de redactar las noticias y se las entregué al locutor para su difusión, escuche un gran ruido, acompañado de gritos pidiendo auxilio mientras trocitos de techo caían sobre mi cabeza; y vi entonces una luz azul, algo así como luz de acetileno, entrando en la habitación y cubriéndolo todo. Creía que nuestra emisora acaba de recibir un impacto.

 Cubriéndome la cabeza con cuidado y temblando temeroso del mundo que me esperaba afuera, corrí hacia la habitación de la sección de programación. ¡Ay! ¡La habitación ya no era la misma! No había habitación a la que entrar ya que la mayoría de escritorios, sillas y demás muebles, así como las ventanas estaban hechas añicos; varios de mis compañeros estaban tendidos en el suelo muy gravemente heridos por la explosión. La sangre brotaba de sus caras y manos; alguien pedía ayuda a gritos con un ojo cortado por un trozo de cristal. Ante esta catástrofe, yo no sabía qué hacer. Un periodista del Dōmei Tsūshinsha (una conocida agencia de noticias japonesa de antes de la guerra) entró corriendo, desnudo, y me pidió algo para ponerse encima. Le di un uniforme kaki que estaba allí tirado. Corrí luego a mi escritorio donde encontré mi sombrero, mi traje y una mochila con lo necesario para casos de emergencia.

Momentos más tarde, todos los trabajadores recogían sus ropas y pertenencias y se preparaban para salir corriendo a pesar de sus heridas en la cabeza, manos o pies; algunos habían huido ya a lugares más seguros. Se inició un fuego en una esquina de la emisora pero fue contenido a tiempo.

Miré afuera por la ventana rota, ¡Ay! Todas las casas de madera a la vista se habían desmoronado o estaban echas añicos y se veía a lo lejos el humo y el fuego avanzando. Me pregunté qué habría pasado. En la calle anterior a la de la emisora de radio, vi a mucha gente gravemente herida, hombres, mujeres y niños en agonía. Y de sus caras, manos y pechos vi brotar sangre. Los niños gritaban en vano el nombre de sus padres y hermanos desaparecidos. Algunos corrían por las calles sin ropa que cubriese sus cuerpos heridos. Cuando vi lo que sufría la gente, me acordé de algunos de los terribles pasajes y escenas del *Paraiso Perdido* del Inferno de Dante, que leí cuando era joven.

Me di cuenta de que toda la ciudad había sido destruida, pero no alcanzaba a comprender cómo podía haber pasado todo aquello en tan solo un momento; era un misterio; y nadie sabía la verdad en aquel momento; sólo llegábamos a la vaga conclusión de que una poderosa bomba había caído o que alguna fuerza eléctrica especial había sacudido la ciudad y los suburbios.

En medio de esta catástrofe, sin embargo, volví en mí y encontré la manera de llegar a un refugio más seguro. Pensé primero en mi madre, enferma, y en mi único hijo, en la fábrica, pero el fuego cortaba ya la ciudad en dos y no podía llegar hasta ellos. ¡Qué Dios los proteja! Recogí mi traje y mi mochila y decidí cruzar el puente Sakae, el más cercano a la emisora, y dirigirme al "East Drill Ground." De camino a la salida me encontré con una locutora, la señorita Izawa, tendida en el suelo e incapaz de caminar debido a sus heridas en un pie. Con ayuda de unos compañeros, la llevamos hasta la entrada donde encontramos al señor Majima, jefe de la sección de programas, con el cuerpo ensangrentado y pidiendo ayuda.

Varias personas gritaban pidiendo auxilio. Una mujer me agarró de la mano y me pidió que salvara a su padre, atrapado bajo unas vigas. Y un niño de unos dos años lloraba buscando a su madre. Yo no sabía qué hacer. Decidí primero ayudar a la locutora y al jefe. Coloqué una tabla sobre un cochecito de bebé que había encontrado en la entrada y, con la ayuda de mis compañeros, los tumbamos sobre ella. Pero pesaban demasiado y la tabla se rompió al instante dejando caer a los heridos al suelo. El jefe se quedó al cuidado de mis compañeros y yo llevé a la locutora en brazos, auque con mucha dificultad pues, pesaba demasiado y el calor era muy intenso. Además, el camino estaba lleno de vigas caídas, tuberías y piedras.

Caminé dos manzanas con la mujer a cuestas, tropezando y cayendo al suelo dos o tres veces. No había demasiada gente en la calle y me di cuenta que se habían originado incendios en varios lugares cerca de donde estábamos. Me detuve delante de las puertas de la mansión del señor Awaya, administrador jefe del distrito de Chugoku. Observé los gruesos muros de la casa y el tanque de agua y me pareció que este sería el lugar más seguro para refugiarnos y así se lo hice saber a la señorita Izawa. Le pedí que no se moviese de allí hasta que regresase con un vehículo. Aunque pareció cruel dejarla allí, no tenía alternativa, el peligro nos acechaba por todos lados.

Al poco tiempo de dejarla, me enteré después, se vio rodeada por el fuego y se vio obligada a meterse en el tanque de agua y pasar allí la noche entera en compañía de otra mujer que también se había refugiado dentro. Al día siguiente, fue rescatada por un coche del departamento de comunicación del Hospital de Hiroshima y llevada al hospital donde fue curada. Su padre murió aquel día y su madre fue herida. Ella se recuperó y hoy trabaja en una imprenta de Hiroshima y vive con su madre. En el primer aniversario conmemorativo de la caída de la bomba atómica, me llamó y me dio las gracias con un cuenco de arroz. ¡Qué encuentro tan feliz fue aquél!

Cuando me separé de la mujer, corrí hacia el puente. En el camino me encontré de nuevo con el señor Majima, tendido en el suelo. Su mujer estaba a su lado y me pidió que los ayudara. Afortunadamente vi al señor Date (que moriría más adelante) corriendo por la calle. Le pedí que me ayudara y, tras colocarlo sobre un tablón, lo cargamos entre los dos. Caminamos una manzana hasta dar con una casa destrozada con un amplio jardín. Pensamos que este podría ser un refugio seguro, así que entramos y lo dejamos en una esquina del jardín. Ahora el fuego avanzaba por dos frentes distintos y el señor Date y yo nos despedimos del jefe y su mujer.

¿Qué le pasó al señor Majima después? Cuando, dos días después, regresé al lugar en el que nos habíamos separado, no había ni rastro de él; quizá alguna partida de rescate lo enterró en algún lugar. En cuanto a su mujer, ella me contó que su marido falleció a los cinco minutos de separarnos; ella se marchó con la hija del administrador jefe que pasaba por allí, al río y, desde allí, a la comisaría de policía. Después llegó al "East Drill Ground" donde pasó dos noches antes de dirigirse a la casa de una amiga íntima en el lado oeste de la ciudad. Ella es la hija del señor Iwao Kongo, un conocido músico japonés, el cantante de "Noh Song."

Después de separarme de mi jefe y de su mujer, llegué, con mucha dificultad, al puente, pero no pude cruzarlo ya que todas las casas a su alrededor estaban en llamas. Detrás de mí se originó otro fuego y decidí saltar hacia los bancos de arena del río. Perdí la mochila en el agua y la vi flotando no muy lejos. Dudé por un instante, pero aquella mochila y sus partencias (documentos bancarios, algo de ropa y comida y otras cosas importantes) eran todo lo que quedaba en este mundo, así que salté al agua y nadé durante tres minutos hasta rescatarla.

Me senté en la arena a pensar qué debía hacer ahora. No tenía ninguna buena idea ni un plan que seguir. Me encontré, bajo el puente, a unos 200 refugiados, la mayoría de ellos con ropas ensangrentadas y gravemente heridos. Estaban descalzos y no tenían nada más que lo puesto. Cinco militares aparecieron llevando una bandera reglamentaria. Un teniente se me acercó y me pidió que le vendara su mano herida. Sangraba mucho y como no tenía nada con que vendarla, rasgué mi camisa blanca y la até alrededor de su mano. Él me lo agradeció mucho. Al cabo de un rato, los militares encontraron un pequeño bote y se dirigieron río arriba. El viento avivaba con fuerza el fuego y pronto cenizas y trozos de madera volaron hasta donde estábamos nosotros, obligándonos a saltar al río con frecuencia para protegernos. Tenía hambre, pues no había comido nada desde el desayuno. Encontré un trozo de cebolla flotando en río. Lo cogí y me lo comí acompañado por un puñado de arroz crudo que tenía en la mochila. En un momento de urgencia, cualquier cosa satisface el estómago.

Sobre las 10 de la mañana, las oscuras nubes que cubrían el cielo dejaron escapar la lluvia que lavaba, ahora, las caras de los miserables refugiados. Escuchamos el sonido constante de las explosiones y, temiendo ser bombardeados, la gente empezó a correr en todas direcciones. El fuego se extendía por todas partes. Yo me sentía muy solo pesando que el final estaba cerca. Por suerte, el agua del río empezaba a descender, dejando a la vista más bancos de arena por los que poder caminar. Sabía que a menos de medio kilómetro se encontraba la comisaría este de policía, así que empecé a caminar por los bancos de arena.

CAPÍTULO 2

EN LAS MONTAÑAS

"Cuando una puerta se cierra, una ventana se abre."

—PROVERBIO ITALIANO

AMINÉ POR LA ARENA, A VECES TENIENDO QUE SALTAR. El fuego consumía toda la ciudad y no se apagaría en todo el día. El humo y el calor cubrían cielo y tierra. Escuchaba el sonido de las casas resquebrajándose y veía los árboles ardiendo y quebrándose, emitiendo destellos como en una corriente eléctrica. Observé el humo en las montañas sobre la ciudad. El cruel sol brillaba sobre las cabezas de la pobre gente. Vi en las arenas del río a muchos refugiados, heridos y con el espíritu roto, compañeros y amigos ayudándolos, vendando sus heridas como podían; un bebé muriendo en los brazos de su madre; los semblantes sin esperanza, esperando lo peor. ¿Adónde podían ir? ¿Dónde podrían estar ahora las tías, hermanos y resto de seres queridos? ¿Cómo conseguirían provisiones para los siguientes días?

"No estoy tranquilo, ni callado, y tampoco he descansado, pero se avecinan problemas."

No podía dejar de quejarme.

Me subí a un banco de arena del río. Vi muchos muertos aquí y allí; hombres y mujeres; jóvenes y viejos; niños y bebés y también perros y gatos; algunos con las caras quemadas; otros con los cuerpos desnudos y cortados, con la piel oscurecida por el humo y el fuego. No podía soportar ver aquellas formas miserables. El olor de la muerte mezclado con el del humo impregnaba el aire y las calles.

De pie, sobre lo alto del banco, miré alrededor. Incendio tras incendio; demolición tras demolición. ¡Hiroshima, nuestra querida ciudad, arde! Nuestro querido hogar se desvanece por completo. Todo está perdido. Se acabó Hiroshima; arde el este y arde el oeste, incendios por todas partes. Hace mucho calor. La gente ha perdido la vida y ha sido enterrada; las casas se caen; los tranvías y los coches se consumen por las llamas. Al oeste de donde me encontraba vi cómo las crueles llamas salían de las ventanas del edificio de prensa Chugoku y de los colosales grandes almacenes Fukuya. La cruz de la torre más alta de la iglesia metodista, a donde solía acudir los domingos, estaba humeante. Sólo los edificios de cemento conservaban su forma y estructura, a pesar de que, en su interior, los muebles y demás objetos habrían sido reducidos a cenizas. Supe que nuestra emisora resistiría a pesar de los incendios del interior, pues se trataba de un edificio de cemento.

Finalmente llegué a la comisaría este, pero no había nadie de servicio; varios policías yacían en el suelo. En una esquina, encontré agua fresca corriendo de una tubería rota. Bebí. Con el calor y la sed que tenía, bebí varios vasos de aquella agua refrescante. Cerca de la oficina, había varias bicicletas a punto de quemarse. Decidí tomar una prestada, sin permiso, porque no había a nadie al que poder preguntar. ¡Que Dios me perdone! La necesitaba para escapar del fuego y del peligro. Así que monté y pedaleé con todas mis fuerzas por la parte este de la ciudad, a través de calles en llamas y atravesando puentes humeantes.

Por fin llegué, no sin dificultad, al "Eastern Drill Ground", donde me encontré con grupos de refugiados descansando sobre el suelo seco, fatigados, heridos, casi desnudos y despojados de toda posesión. La gente llevaba a hombros a los heridos más graves.

Me tumbé en la hierba y miré hacia el cielo, respirando el aire fresco. Después de respirar el humo de la ciudad, sentaba bien respirar aquel aire limpio. Me sentí cansado y pesaba qué hacer a continuación. Recordé que nos habían dicho que en caso de que nuestro estudio fuera destruido, nos encontraríamos en la emisora Hara, situada a tres kilómetros al norte. Pero el camino directo, a través de la calle Yokoyawa, había sido cortado por el fuego. Decidí entonces, rodear la aldea Hara por el este. Si tomaba el camino de las montañas y cruzaba el río, llegaría a la emisora Hara.

Y eso es lo que hice. Sentí un poco de esperanza en mi corazón. El lugar donde había descansado estaba en los suburbios del este de Hiroshima. A pesar de que las casas de alrededor estaban lejos de la ciudad, algunas estaban en llamas y los tejados y ventanas de la mayoría estaban hechos añicos e incluso había casas que se habían caído… Había heridos aquí y allí pidiendo ayuda. Algunas personas habían salido ilesas y yo di gracias a Dios por encontrarme a salvo.

Descansé durante media hora y me puse de nuevo en marcha, colina arriba. Eran las dos de la tarde. Tenía hambre. Pasé por delante de una casa y me dirigí hacia la entrada sin saber quién vivía allí; una mujer mayor y una chica se encontraban allí. Había también muchos refugiados en todas las habitaciones. Les conté cómo había escapado de la ciudad en llamas y les dije que quería descasar un rato. Me llevaron a una habitación y me ofrecieron amablemente tarta y té. Cocine yo mismo algo de arroz que tenía en mi mochila junto con unas patatas que la mujer me había dado. Después de comer, me despedí de ellas y de nuevo monté la bicicleta colina arriba. De camino, vi varios camiones del ejército transportando heridos colina arriba. La mayoría de ellos estaban casi desnudos o con las ropas ensangrentadas; las caras y cabellos quemados así que no pude distinguir si eran hombres o mujeres.

Lentamente, uno de los coches se acercó a mi. Eché un vistazo y vi a un noble oficial tendido con la cara herida. Luego me enteré de que era un príncipe coreano al servicio de la armada y que había sido gravemente herido cerca del puente de Aigi, el epicentro de la explosión atómica, cuado montaba su caballo. Los hombres encargados de su protección, sintiéndose culpables por no haber estado cerca de su amo, se suicidaron. También pasé por delante de una escuela de primaria en la que también muchos refugiados hacinados recibían atención médica y unas raciones de galletas y arroz.

La pendiente de la colina era ahora demasiado empinada, así que desmonté de la bicicleta y seguí a pie. Un camión lleno de heridos pasó a mi lado y fue entonces cuando escuche la voz de una mujer llamándome,

"¡Señor Ozaki! ¡Señor Ozaki!"

"¿Quién eres?" pregunté.

"Yamazaki, oficial de la emisora de radio. Me hirieron gravemente en la espalda", me dijo ella.

Se encontraba sentada en el medio del coche, vestida tan solo con dos trozos de tela y un semblante triste.

"¡Ten cuidado y que Dios te ayude! Me aseguraré de contarle al encargado lo que te pasó. Por favor, aguanta."

El camión aceleró y se perdió en la distancia. Ella se recuperaría después de recibir tratamiento médico y hora sigue trabajando en nuestra emisora.

Me encontré con dos chicas que trabajaban en las oficinas de la emisora, una de ellas caminaba apoyada en una vara. Les pregunté cómo habían llegado hasta aquí y ellas me contaron que habían corrido hasta el río y que, allí, habían podido subirse a un pequeño bote y habían llegado hasta allí cruzando la colina de Ushida. Las felicité y luego tomamos caminos diferentes, pues ellas iban a casa de unos amigos cerca de la aldea.

Una hora después llegué al río. Tenía que cruzarlo. Había un pequeño ferry que maniobraba un chico. Amablemente nos llevó a mi y a mi bicicleta a la otra orilla. Le pedí que me cobrara el pasaje.

"¿El pasaje? ¿Cree que puedo pedirle dinero a los refugiados? Usted viene de Hiroshima, supongo. ¿Cómo voy a pedirle dinero a un refugiado? Es mi deber ayudar".

Aquello me conmovió profundamente y notaba como mis ojos se humedecían. ¡El sabía cómo la gente del país estaba sufriendo!

Estaba anocheciendo. Pregunté a unos aldeanos por la emisora Hara y me dijeron que estaba a menos de veinte minutos. Me pasó un camión cargado con provisiones que se dirigía a Hiroshima y alguien me tiró un paquete desde dentro. Eran unas galletas. Se lo agradecí como regalo del cielo. A las seis y media de la tarde, llegué sano y salvo a la emisora. Unos diez de mis compañeros estaban ya allí esperando al resto. Todo el mundo estaba un poco aturdido. El encargado estaba allí y le conté toda mi experiencia con detenimiento. Los compañeros me dieron la bienvenida y me ofrecieron una toalla y otras cosas y me sirvieron un plato de arroz caliente y sopa.

Me di cuenta que, a pesar de que se encontraba a cinco kilómetros de Hiroshima, la emisora también había sido dañada por la bomba, con las ventanas rotas y los techos caídos debido a la honda expansiva. Entonces comprendí cuan grandes habían sido los efectos de aquella bomba atómica. La emisora tenía un jardín alrededor de la oficina. Salí, en la oscuridad y vi cómo algunas plantas empezaban a florecer. Todo estaba inmóvil. En el cielo, a ocho kilómetros al sur de allí, vi un gran fuego, tan brillante como el día, devorando ferozmente la ciudad.

¡Era Hiroshima! Nuestra querida ciudad y hogar. Me arrodillé en la hierba y recé a Dios por la seguridad de mi madre, que estaba en su casa, y por mi único hijo, Sei-ichi, que estaba trabajando en una fábrica cerca de la ciudad, y por mis amigos y sus familias que todavía no habían sido encontrados. ¿Era este el final de Hiroshima? ¿Y de mi vida? Recé; sentí que Dios me ayudaba. A pesar de la catástrofe y de la mala fortuna, Dios estaba conmigo. Quedaban todavía habitaciones en las que vivir, refugios en los que resguardarse a este lado de Japón. El desastre me hizo más fuerte. Y recordé los versículos de las Escrituras —

"Tenemos también Gloria en el sufrimiento; sabiendo que el sufrimiento ataca nuestra paciencia; la paciencia a la experiencia y la experiencia a la esperanza—"

¡Sí! ¡Experiencia y esperanza! El viento frío me despertó de mi meditación; entré de nuevo, preparado para dormir sobre unas mantas en el suelo. Pero no puede dormir ni un poco, y pasé la noche en vela, inquieto en cuerpo y mente.

CAPÍTULO 3

EN BUSCA DE MIS
SERES QUERIDOS

*"Es obvio que, las circunstancias por sí solas no nos hacen felices o infelices.
Nuestros sentimientos están determinados por la manera que reaccionamos ante ellos.
Todos podemos resistir ante el desastre y triunfar sobre él – si tenemos que hacerlo.
Somos más fuertes de lo que pensamos."*

— DALE CARNEGIE

ME LEVANTÉ CON LOS OJOS SOMNOLIENTOS Y EL CUERPO ENTUMECIDO. El hombre puede encontrar fácilmente el camino en tiempos normales, pero es difícil saber qué hacer ante extraordinarias y urgentes circunstancias. Y cuando la gente está perdida ante el desastre, no puede ni reaccionar. Volvimos en sí con el viento frío de la mañana, y empezamos a pensar cuál debía ser nuestro primer paso ese día. Lo primero que teníamos que hacer era comunicar a la emisora de radio de Tokio lo que había sucedido. La mayor parte de las líneas habían sido destruidas en la explosión, aunque encontramos una red todavía en pie que comunicaba Hiroshima y Tokio a través de la ciudad de Himeji. Así que mandamos un breve informe diciendo: "la ciudad ha sido destruida en el ataque aéreo, nuestra emisora ha ardido, hay muchos trabajadores muertos y grandes daños materiales, etc." Había mucho que hacer en la emisora. Mientras esperábamos ayuda de las emisoras vecinas, nuestro siguiente paso fue la búsqueda de los trabajadores desaparecidos y de nuestras familias.

Así, dejé la emisora y pedaleé de nuevo hacia Hiroshima en busca de mi familia. La carretera estaba llena de gente, caminando desde y hacia la ciudad; heridos, gente cargando pesadas bolsas, coches, carruajes y camiones repletos de refugiados; algunos agitados por los recientes acontecimientos, otros dejándose caer por la fatiga y el calor del verano. Llegué a Yokogawa, la entrada a la ciudad. Había un camión con comida y provisores; alguien me llamó y me dio una ración de arroz. A partir de aquí, el camino se hizo más difícil con la bicicleta ya que varios postes eléctricos, casas caídas, vigas y piedras interrumpían el camino y la mayor parte de los puentes se habían caído o quemado. No pude ir a mi casa directamente, por el camino habitual. Tuve que dar un rodeo, cambiando de dirección constantemente, a veces incluso teniendo que atravesar los, todavía, humeantes puentes. Tropecé varias veces pero tenía que llegar como fuera al puente del este, cerca de mi casa. Vi, tirados en las calles o flotando en los ríos, muchos cadáveres. Escuché, cerca de la estación de telefonía del oeste, el murmullo débil de la gente en un refugio antiaéreo. Me asomé y encontré a varias chicas desnudas, gravemente heridas y con la piel quemada, abrazadas las unas a las otras como si fueran a morir si se movían. Escuché a una chica llamando con voz débil: "¡Madre! ¡Madre!" Le pregunté su nombre pero no me contestó. No podía ayudarlas porque no había forma de salvarlas. Así que cerré los ojos y recé por ellas. Cerca de allí, una mujer, con un bebé en brazos, caminaba con los ojos llenos de lágrimas. Comprendí que el bebé había muerto.

Finalmente llegué a mi casa, cerca del puente y la encontré convertida en cenizas. Esta fue la peor experiencia de mi vida. Empecé a rebuscar entre las cenizas y los escombros temiendo que, en alguna parte debajo de ellos, encontraría los restos de mi madre, cuando escuché una voz detrás de mi—

"La abuela está a salvo."

Me sorprendí al oírlo. Era mi hijo, sano y salvo. Nos abrazamos con lágrimas en los ojos y dimos gracias a Dios. Él me contó lo siguiente: había escuchado la explosión en la fábrica y había sido derribado por la honda expansiva, pero no herido. Había corrido a toda prisa a casa, que se encontraba a unos veinte minutos de la fábrica, para encontrársela en llamas. La abuela estaba en la puerta con los vecinos. Había encontrado un carruaje, así que montó a la abuela y los vecinos y se marcharon lo más rápido posible hacia la aldea más cercana al otro lado del río. Unos veinte minutos más tarde, un camión de la reserva los recogió y los llevó al pueblo pesquero de Jigogen, a diez kilómetros de la ciudad. Y ahora se encontraban refugiados en una escuela primaria.

Me alegré mucho al escuchar el relato de mi hijo e inmediatamente decidí ir allí y ver a mi madre. Entrada la tarde, llegué a Jigogen, a pie. Los barracones de la escuela estaban a rebosar de refugiados. Encontré a mi madre descansando sobre una colchoneta en un rincón, aturdida y herida en el pie izquierdo. Se alegró de verme sano y salvo.

Nos sirvieron sopa y arroz y nos dieron algo de ropa. Como las habitaciones de la escuela estaban abarrotadas y la gente estaba muriendo, decidimos pasar la noche en el suelo. Pero con los trastornos de los recientes acontecimientos y las picaduras de los mosquitos, no conseguimos dormir.

CAPÍTULO 4

LA CIUDAD QUEMADA

"Sufriendo, el hombre aprende."

— BLAISE PASCAL

E L OCTAVO DÍA DE AGOSTO AMANECIÓ CON UN SOL BRILLANTE. Dejé a mi madre y a mi hijo al cuidado de los oficiales al mando y me despedí de ellos, pues tenía muchas cosas que hacer en la emisora.

Llegué al centro de la ciudad. ¡Ay, estaba desierto! La gente lo llamaba ya el desierto atómico, sin habitantes ni árboles, ni rastro de vida. Los tranvías ardían aquí y allí. El olor a muerte impregnaba las calles. El puente de Aioi, de hierro y cemento, estaba roto, el hierro doblado y las paredes destrozadas. Escuché que unos 200 trabajadores fueron sepultados en un momento en la oficina de correos de Hiroshima y que tan solo dos o tres habían sobrevivido; y que unos 600 oficiales de la prefactura del gobierno habían corrido la misma suerte. Los pasajeros que viajaban en tranvía perdieron la vida en un instante aquel día. Sin duda, uno de los mayores sacrificios en vidas de la Historia.

Me detuve delante de los grandes almacenes Fukuya. Las luces brillantes y los murmullos alegres de las muchachas habían desaparecido; sólo quedaba el fuego y el humo. Llegué al cruce donde estaba el banco Kangyo para encontrarme con una multitud de heridos graves en el suelo del banco, la mayoría con la cara quemada y todos gritando y llorando. Médicos y enfermeras los atendían, vendando y curando sus heridas.

Finalmente llegué a la emisora. El nuevo suelo de madera ya no existía, pero el edificio se mantenía en pie. Entré por la puerta principal: todos los aparatos de emisión y archivadores estaban rotos y los muebles, libros y documentos convertidos en ceniza. El agua salía de algunas tuberías rotas, inundando la habitación. Entré en la sección de programación; todo, menos los objetos metálicos, estaba hecho cenizas y el espacio me pareció más grande que nunca. Encontré de casualidad una cajita de lata que solía utilizar y me la guardé como recuerdo. Después fui al refugio antiaéreo y encontré todas las cosas importantes, personales y oficiales, quemadas o llenas de agua. Subí hasta el tejado de la emisora y miré a mi alrededor. Era un desierto, nada quedaba a excepción de algunos edificios de cemento y algunos árboles a medio quemar. Las montañas de Hijiyama parecían estar muy cerca.

De camino a la emisora de Hara, paré a visitar el Viejo Castillo, donde el ejército había establecido su base. No quedaba ni castillo ni barracón militar alguno. Los restos y piedras del castillo dejaban entrever el sueño de un pasado militar brillante. El ejército y el feudalismo habían desaparecido. Deambulé un rato por la hierba quemada, recordando el pasado.

Por la tarde, regresé a la emisora Hara. Les pedimos a los agricultores que nos dejasen utilizar unas habitaciones cercanas a la radio para instalar a nuestros trabajadores. A pesar de que treinta y cinco de ellos habían muerto, toda la sección de programación había resultado ilesa o con heridas leves, aunque muchos de ellos habían perdido a sus mujeres e hijos.

Había muchos rumores a cerca de la gran bomba que cayó sobre Hiroshima. El ministerio de guerra de Japón simplemente dijo que una poderosa bomba había causado grandes daños humanos y materiales en Hiroshima. Más adelante nos enteramos, gracias a la información que captábamos de los Estados Unidos, que había sido la bomba atómica la que había causado el gran desastre y, comprendimos entonces, que la radiación era la causante de la mayor parte de muertos y heridos.

Decían que ninguna forma de vida podría sobrevivir en Hiroshima durante setenta y cinco años, así que la gente que se encontraba en los refugios o en sus casa caídas, empezaron a mudarse a otras partes del país. A decir verdad, el porcentaje de muertes se iba incrementando; la gente que había sido expuesta a la radiación notaban como el pelo se les empezaba a caer y como les empezaban a aparecer manchas en la piel. Morían día a día. Algunos murieron por infecciones que la radiación causó en la sangre. Y como los crematorios de la ciudad habían sido destruidos, las mismas familias desconsoladas tuvieron que incinerar a sus seres queridos.

A los pocos días del ataque a Hiroshima, la gran noticia que se discutía en todo el mundo era la caída de la segunda bomba atómica sobre Nagasaki, y la declaración de guerra de Rusia a Japón, que empezó con el ataque de los rusos a la frontera de Manchuria. Desgracia tras desgracia. ¿Cómo podíamos resistir tal ataque? Los días de Japón estaban contados. El ejército y la marina ya no tenían control sobre Japón ni sobre los japoneses.

Nos informaron que Japón estaba negociando la paz con las fuerzas aliadas. El 15 de agosto nos dijeron que el Emperador daría, a las doce en punto, un terrible mensaje y que todo el mundo debía escucharlo. Nosotros estábamos muy ocupados intentando emitir este boletín informativo. La gente de nuestro país había esperado ansiosa e impaciente este momento.

Ese día todo el mundo detuvo lo que estaba haciendo para escuchar atentamente la radio. Cuando la voz del Emperador se escuchó, supimos que el último día de guerra había llegado. Pero, ¡rendición incondicional! No puedo expresar con este bolígrafo las impresiones vividas en aquel momento histórico; cómo nos sentimos y lo que pasaría en esta tierra después. Todos lloramos; lloramos con sentimientos encontrados. Los hombres de servicio volvieron a casa. La gente que, durante la guerra, se habían marchado a las aldeas, se preparó para regresar a casa o a las ciudades quemadas; y los trenes y barcos llenos a rebosar, los traían de vuelta. Hubo desorden en las calles durante algún tiempo, hasta que las fuerzas aliadas llegaron a esta orilla.

Mi madre, que había regresado a la ciudad y vivía en su casa en ruinas, murió la mañana del 1 de septiembre debido a sus heridas en el pie. Mi hijo y yo echamos gasolina sobre su cuerpo y le prendimos fuego. Parecería cruel hacer eso, pero no podíamos hacer otra cosa en aquel momento. Dios lo sabe. Para enterrar sus restos, me preparaba para regresar a mi pueblo natal, Shikoku, en el mar interior, cuando hubo una inundación, la medianoche del 17 de septiembre. Las lluvias duraron varios días. Me despertaron los gritos a medianoche. "¡Inundación! ¡Inundación!" Abrí la ventana; ¡Ay! El agua llegaba ya al segundo piso de la casa en la que me alojaba. Si el agua llegase a mover la casa, ¿qué pasaría entonces? Sobre la cruel agua vi restos de casas y troncos flotando. No había forma de escapar y solo podíamos esperar a que el agua descendiese con la llegada de la mañana.

Y al romper el alba nos sentimos a salvo. El agua había descendido hasta el medio metro. ¡Inundación tras las llamas! Los daños causados por la inundación afectarían a la recolección de las cosechas y verduras. Nuestros corazones se oscurecieron.

Como tenía los restos de mi madre conmigo en aquella tarde de la inundación, me aventuré con mi hijo hasta el puerto, a unos seis kilómetros al sur. Tuvimos que cruzar fuertes corrientes y con mucha dificultad llegamos a la ciudad al anochecer. Estaba oscura y muerta, completamente deshabitada. Encontramos un tranvía destrozado y nos quedamos dentro a descansar un par de horas. Luego continuamos nuestro camino hacia el puerto. A la mañana siguiente cogimos un pequeño bote hacia mi pueblo natal para enterrar los restos de mi madre.

Un hermoso día de otoño, los soldados de la fuerzas de ocupación llegaron a Kure, ex-puerto naval. ¡El nuevo día había llegado!

LA PAZ HA LLEGADO

*"No pretendemos que los japoneses sean esclavizados como raza ni destruidos
como nación… El gobierno japonés deberá levantar los obstáculos al restablecimiento
y fortalecimiento de las tendencias democráticas entre los japoneses ."*

— DE LA DECLARACIÓN DE POTSDAM

CUATRO AÑOS HAN PASADO DESDE EL DÍA INOLVIDABLE en el que la primera bomba atómica calló sobre la tierra de Hiroshima. Ahora, Japón, donde ya no hay más guerra, ha empezado a dar sus primeros pasos como nación democrática. ¡Todo ha cambiado! ¡El feudalismo japonés ha desaparecido! La nueva Constitución de Japón se firmó el 3 de noviembre de 1947. Y con ella se han garantizado la "libertad de expresión, de religión y pensamiento, así como el respeto a los derechos humanos fundamentales." Los hombres de servicio fueron liberados. Y los soldados en el extranjero, en China, Siberia y los mares del sur regresaron a sus casas quemadas y rotas. El ejército fue desarmado completamente y la soberanía de Japón ha sido limitada a las viejas islas, perdiendo muchas de sus colonias. En consecuencia, la población de postguerra en este pequeño territorio será de unos 80.000.000. Las condiciones sociales fueron muy duras durante un tiempo. La inflación hizo que la vida fuera más dura cada día; los mercados negros crecieron por todas partes. Viviendas, comida y ropa eran escasas y los precios subían a diario. Ladrones y asesinos abarrotaban las celdas de las comisarías. Los días inciertos y las noches sin descanso duraron mucho tiempo. Los jóvenes que habían recibido instrucción militar parecían haber perdido su objetivo en la vida. Y también malinterpretaron el verdadero significado de la Democracia; su modo de vida era poco civilizado y desordenado, deambulando por las calles o en los mercados negros, o cometiendo robos en grupo.

En las librerías, se venden libros y revistas baratos e inmorales. Las amas de casa tienen que ir a las granjas a comprar arroz, maíz y verduras de los granjeros, cambiándolos por sus vestimentas.

Efectivamente, Japón era un crisol de desorden. Las condiciones sociales empezaron a mejorar a finales del tercer año: las fuerzas aliadas, especialmente americanas e inglesas, nos tendieron una mano dándonos comida y ropa. Los bienes que La Administración de Ayuda y Rehabilitación de las Naciones Unidas y la Agencia de Ayuda a Asia distribuían, animaban a los huérfanos, a las viudas y a las personas sin hogar. Las raciones de comida habían aumentado, había suministro de ropa y se empezaban a reconstruir las casas.

¡Esperanza y reconstrucción! Debemos seguir adelante a pesar de los desastres. Hiroshima tiene hoy en día 250.000 habitantes (tenía 312.200 antes de la bomba) y 60.000 casas (de las 76.000 que hubo antes de aquel día). Grandes almacenes, bancos, cines y publicaciones oficiales y privadas han empezado a funcionar otra vez; los tranvías circulan de nuevo; y casas de té caliente, cafés y restaurantes han abierto sus puertas.

Barcos llenos de cargamento vienen del extranjero al puerto de Ujina; y turistas extranjeros vienen diariamente a ver las ruinas de la ciudad atómica, preguntándose cuales fueron los efectos reales de la bomba. Hiroshima está renaciendo. La campaña "No más Hiroshimas" recorre ahora Japón y el mundo entero.

Ahora nos hacemos eco, con alegría y esperanza, de la declaración de la nueva Constitución de Japón a las personas de paz: "el pueblo japonés renuncia para siempre a la guerra como derecho soberano de la nación y al uso de la violencia para solucionar disputas internacionales." Así que no es el último día de Hiroshima, sino que, esperamos, sea el primero.

— FIN —

広島の歌

序文
ノエル・ケイポン

1999年、ロイス・クルーズ氏は、94歳のときにニューヨーク州ロングアイランドにあるポートワシントンで他界した。ロイスの近い親類である私の妻と私は、ロイスの家を売却することにした。彼女の所有物に目を通し、必要なものは残し、それ以外のものはオークションに出すことに決めた。屋根裏を片付けている際、私はノートに書いてある資料を見つけ、数週間後、私はこの資料を読んだ。そして今、ウェセックス社は「広島の歌」を出版している。

　第二次世界大戦以前、ロイスの夫アルバート・クルーズ氏はNBCで働いていた。戦後に、彼はマッカーサー司令官のスタッフとして、放送局の局員にアドバイスするため、広島で数週間過ごした。クルーズ氏は放送局で翻訳とコミュニケーションの担当をしている秘書の尾崎淳博さんから手書きのノートを受け取った。

　1945年8月6日、尾崎さんは原子爆弾が投下された中心から1キロ以内にある広島中央放送局で働いていた。彼がクルーズ氏に渡したノートは、その2、3日の内に彼が何をしたか、何を見たかの記録である。彼がクルーズ氏にノートを渡したのはアメリカにいる人々と自分の体験を分かち合うためである。クルーズ氏がこの資料を使ったのか、それともただポートワシントンの屋根裏部屋に半世紀以上おいてあったのかはわからない。いずれにしても、60年経ったが、このたびの出版はノートを書いた尾崎さんの希望を実現している。

　この記録をより多くの人々に読んでもらえるように、ウェセックスは英語、日本語、スペイン語及び中国語で「広島の歌」を発行している。また、私たちは尾崎さんよりクルーズ氏への手紙及び彼のノート全体を複写した。分かり易く理解できるように、私たちは発行する際に尾崎さんの原本に少しスペルの変更と編集を行った。

　ノエル・ケイポン
　ニューヨーク州　ブロンクスビル
　2011年1月1日

ノエル・ケイポンはニューヨーク州にあるコロンビアビジネススクールの国際マーケティング科R.C.コプフ教授陣の一人である。ディアナ・クーンはニューヨーク州にあるコロンビア大学ティーチャーズカレッジの心理および教育学の教授である

広島の歌

— 1945年8月6日 —

尾崎　淳博

企画部
広島中央放送局
日本国　広島

まえがき

「その中心に大きな苦悩のない時代には、その生活に偉大な音楽も無い」

カール・バルト

　我々が愛する、七つの川の透き通った水が未だ流れる広島の大地と通りに、歴史上初の原子爆弾が投下された、あの忘れがたき日1945年8月6日の4周年記念日があと数カ月で訪れようとしている。今は春である一愛しい人々がかつて散歩をしていた川の両岸には桜が咲き乱れ、空にはヒバリのさえずりが響き、凍て付いた土地から緑が顔を出し始めている。愛しい人々が眠る墓の上に咲く花々は、幾度となく花開きまた消えていった。自然は変わらない、しかし人類は変わってしまった。我々がかつて愛した者たちはもういない、我々の古き家々の、居心地が良い部屋や馴染みのある家具は消えてしまった！

　しかし、神は奪い、また与えたまう。我々のうち何人かは苦難にも関わらず生き続ける希望と強さを持ち続けている。

　あの歴史的瞬間に新しい日が始まった。原子爆弾に残された惨禍と灰の中から、生存者は「恐怖から解放」され、新しき日のために立ち上がった。新設の狭いバラックの窓から、焼け焦げた庭へと明るい光が射し、「広島復興のうた」のメロディーが暗い星空にこだまとなって反響している。

　「広島を建て直そう、さあ夜明けだ、朝だ、我々は喜んでいる、ハンマーの音が朝の風に響き、原子爆弾の荒野から希望が生まれる」

　そうだ！復興と希望。

　まずなぜ私がこの記録を書いているかを説明させてもらいたい。あの忘れがたき日の朝、私は初めての原子爆弾が投下された中心から1キロ以内にある広島中央放送局で働いていた。約35人の私の同僚は亡くなり、市の郊外にある我が家にいた私の愛する母も、重傷を受けた後に他界してしまった。私にいたっては幸い安全で、分厚い壁に囲まれた部屋にいたためひとつの傷もなかった。愛する母、我が家、我が家具、私のお気に入りの本に身の回りの物、それに職場を失うというのは、どれだけ困難な経験であったことか。人類の歴史の記録の中で、結果的にこんなに多くのものが一瞬で失われた惨禍があったのだろうか？

　当時広島には366,000人の住民がいた。初めての原子爆弾により、放射能または倒壊した家に押し潰されて92,133人の市民が死亡し、9,428人が重傷となり、27,997人が軽傷を負い、生存者は176,987人、そして8,200軒の家（市の90%）は焼けて灰となり、放射能による死者は46,185人から70,000人へと日々増えていった。（この数字に軍

隊と救援隊の人数は含まれていない）そして有名な場所や歴史的に貴重な記念物、建造物は消えてしまった！すべて消えた！そして我々の愛する者たちとすべてが、一瞬にして消え去ってしまった。

　嵐は嵐を呼ぶという。この大参事に加えて、約一か月以内の9月17日には、大洪水がまるで幽霊のように日本のこの地方を訪れ多大な被害を与えた。（1,199人が死亡もしくは溺死し、897人が行方不明となり、家や田舎の土地に被害が及んだ。）

　戦後まもなくして、私は職場にて友人達と、拙い文章で思うようにかけないとしても、あのような悲惨な経験と出来事を次の世代への資料として記録するべきだと話していた。

　しかしながら、当時我々は放送局の仕事であったり、新しい家を建てたり生活を立て直したりするのにとても忙しく、約4年間の時間が夢のように過ぎてしまった。しかしそれは夢ではなく事実であり、将来人類の間で闘争や戦争がもう二度とないことの現われであった。

　戦友達が迫害者や独裁者の下で長く苦しんだこの封建的な国に平和が来たのだ！新しい時代が本当に来たのだ！私は、この両目で見てこの両耳で聞き、私の存在そのもの全てで経験したあの日の事を日記か記録として書き留めなければならない。これは我が国と世界中の平和を愛する人々のための私の義務である。

　　私は日本のために
　　日本は世界のために
　　世界はキリストのために
　　そして全ては神のために
　　　　　— 内村　鑑三

　事実これは、最初の原子爆弾が市に投下された朝に起こった真実と強烈な出来事を記録することを意図した、人類の証書である。しかしながら、私の拙い英語の知識では私の経験した事を鮮明に描くことができないのではないかと懸念している。しかし、事実を語ることそのものが、何が起こったかを真に証明するものと心得ている。科学的なことや医学的な研究は他に任せ、私の目的は私の個人的な体験のみを記録することである。

　私にいたっては、関西学院大学、アメリカ人宣教師ラムブレス博士によって設立されたメソジスト教会大学を卒業後、牧師、英語教師、新聞記者を経て、現在は広島中央放送局ラジオ放送局の仕事に従事し、原子爆弾の焼け野原にあるささやかな小屋に住み新しい日本の日々の生活を楽しんでいる一介の市民である。

　尾崎　淳博
　1949年　5月

第1章

あの日

「クリスチャンの喜びは困難により増す」

― ピーク

あれは1945年8月6日のことであった。暑く照りつける日々が続いていたが、アメリカ戦闘機の空襲が昼夜問わず繰り返され、1944年末までには最も重要な地点や都市は崩壊または焼かれ灰となり、すでに東京とその郊外は数々の攻撃を受け多大な被害を被っていた。アメリカはマリアナ諸島を占領し、そこから戦闘機B29が我々の都市や重要な地点を自由に攻撃した。1945年1月3日、名古屋に戦闘機が90機到来し、台湾と沖縄は攻撃され、500機の航空母艦から爆撃を受けた。1月30日には、アメリカの陸軍と海軍はマニラを攻めることを試み、2月16日、米国の艦隊が硫黄島に着陸し、史上最も残酷な戦役がはじまった。3月16日には大阪、3月17日には神戸が、それぞれ攻撃を受け二つの都市は火の海と化した。そして同月の21日には、多くの犠牲と双方の過酷の戦いのすえ、ついに硫黄島はアメリカ軍任務部隊に占領された。この頃までには最も重要な都市とこれらの島々の基地はB29や輸送機により攻撃され、家々や重要な地点は破壊され焼き払われ、人々は家も、服も、食べ物も無くさまよった。さまよえる羊はどこへ行くことができようか？苦難に満ちた生活の中の日本はただ戦敗の苦しみを味わうほか何もできなかった。

このような報告やニュースを受け我々は憂鬱な気分になり、迎えるであろう悲劇的な運命と暗い日々を段々と認識し始めていた。政府の指導者達は人々に最終的な勝利を信じ込ませようと務めたが、実際にはむなしい叫びであった。

あの日は朝から暑かった。当時私が放送局で担当していた仕事は防衛空軍の通信で、広島と呉の陸海軍基地から敵機がどこにあるかの情報を受け、急いで大まかな情報内容を書き上げた後に、私のそばで待つアナウンサーにその原稿を放送のために手渡していた。この仕事は朝から晩まで休みなく、常に神経質に電話を対応することを2年間ほど続けた。

あの日の午前2時に空襲警報が流れ、2，3機の飛行機が広島区域上空を旋回した、しかし午前6時には敵機は依然として広島付近にいたものの、その空襲警報は解かれた。これは基地の責任を司る上官の誤解であった。空襲警報が解かれたことで前夜に市外に逃れた人々や防空壕にいた人々はそれぞれの家に戻り、朝食を摂ったり会社や工場に行く支度をしたりしていた。何人かの人々はすでに市街や庭に出て、前夜の恐怖と疲労の後、朝の爽やかな風に元気づけられていた。日本の通常の暑い夏の習慣どおり、特

に屋内にいる男性や男の子は服を着ず裸、もしくは簡単な浴衣を身に付けるか短パン姿であった。

　まさにあの瞬間、時計の針が8時15分を刺そうとした時、歴史上初の原子爆弾が広島の地に投下された！爆心地は市のほぼ中心の相生橋付近であった。幸い私は、軍の基地からの電話が大きな音で鳴り（あれはだいたい8時であった）防衛空軍通信室に情報を受け取る2人のアナウンサーと共に駆け込んでいた。ニュース原稿を書き上げて担当アナウンサーに渡した時に、助けを呼ぶ人々の叫びとともに巨大な音を聞き、同時に天井のかけらが私の頭に落ちてきた。そして私はアセチレン光のような何か青い閃光が部屋に入り部屋全体を覆うのを見た。私は放送局が直撃を受けたのだと感じた。

　私は椅子にあったクッションで頭を覆い、何がどうなるかわからない恐怖に震えながら企画部の部屋へと駆け込んだ。なんということであろうか！部屋はすっかり変わっていた！ほとんどの机や椅子、他の家具や窓ガラスは壊れ落ち、足を踏み込む隙間はなかった。何人かの私の同僚は顔や体に爆撃による重傷を負って倒れていた。彼らの顔や手からは血が噴き出し、ある人は爆発によってガラスで目を切られ、助けを求めて叫んでいた。この災難の中私は何をしていいのかわからなかった。同盟通信社のとある新聞記者が私に裸で駆け寄ってきて何か着る物をと求めた。そこで私はたまたまそこにあったカーキ色の服を彼に与えた。私は自分の机へと急ぎ、幸い私の帽子、スーツ、それに緊急時に備えた身の回りの物を入れたリュックサックを見つけた。

　一瞬にして、そこにいた全ての同僚は、頭や手や足に重傷を負っているにも関わらず服と身の回りの物を手に取り逃げる準備をしていた。何人かはすでにどこかより安全な場所へと逃げていた。部署の角から急に火が上がったが、ポンプで消火された。

　私は壊れた窓から外を見た。なんということか！私の視界にある全ての木造の家並は倒壊もしくはバラバラに崩壊し、すでにどこからともなく火と煙が上っていた。何が起こったのかを考えた。ラジオ放送局の前の通りで、多くの市民がほぼ裸もしくはシャツや短パンのみでひどい重傷を負ったまま、市の北側へと集団もしくは一人で走っているのを見た。親友や友人たちは重傷を負った男女を互いに助け運び合い、子供達は痛みに苦しんだ。そして彼らの顔や手や胸から、血が噴き出しているのを見た。子供達はいなくなった両親や兄弟の名をむなしく叫んでいた。何人かは重傷を負った体に何の服もまとわずに走っていた。人々がこの惨禍に苦しむ姿を見て、私は若いころに読んだ「失楽園」に描かれたダンテの大火災の悲惨な文章や情景を回想した。

　私は市の全てが倒壊していることを認識した、しかしなぜ一瞬にしてそのような恐ろしく悲惨な結果となったのかが理解できず、謎であった。そしてその緊迫した瞬間に真実を知る者は無く、とても強力で大きな爆弾が投下されたのであろう、もしくは何らかの科学的な方法で特別電流波が市内と郊外に行き渡ったのだろう、というあいまいな結論に達するのみであった。

　このような惨事の中ではあったが、私は我に返り、この危険な場所から別の安全な避難所へと移動する手段を考案した。まず私は病気の母の事と工場にいる私の一人息子の事を考えたが、市のその地域ではすでに火の手が上がっておりそこに戻ることはできなかった。神よ、彼らを守りたまえ！そこで私は駅に一番近い榮橋を渡り、東練兵場に行くことに決めた。決断をしてから、私は急いでスーツを着こみリュックサックの準備をした。1階に降りる途中で、女性アナウンサーの井沢さんが足に打撲を受けて歩けなくなり床に横たわっているのを発見した。私は友人たちと彼女を門まで運び、そこで企画部副部長の間島さんが血まみれの体で横たわり、助けを求め、何人かに囲まれているのを見つけた。

　その時ある女の子が私の手を取り、木材の下敷きになって押しつぶされ動けなくなった父親を助けてくれと頼み、同時に何人かの友人も助けを求めて叫んでいた。2歳くらいの女の子が門の近くでいなくなった母親を探して泣き叫んでいた。私は何をすべきかわからず喪失感にかられた。しかし私はまず、女性アナウンサーと上司を助けることに決め、友人の助けで門の近くで幸い見つけた乳母車に板を載せ、2人を寝かせた。しかし彼らは重過ぎて板はすぐに割れてしまい、重傷を負った2人は地面に落ちてしまった。そこで私は上司の世話を友人に任せ女性アナウンサーを肩に背負った。しかし彼女は重過ぎ、夏の日の熱は厳しく、彼女を背負って歩くことは困難であった。そのうえ、路上は崩れ落ちた梁や柱、壊れた石でいっぱいであった

　私は彼女を背負い、彼女が重過ぎたためよろめき、つまずきながら2区画ほど歩いた。この時何人かが走って逃げており、いくつかの近場から火の手が上がっていた。我々は中国地方長の粟谷さんの豪邸の門前で立ち止まった。私はその豪邸の壁が厚く頑強であること、さらに門の横に雨水貯水槽があることを発見した。私はこの場所がしばらくは彼女にとって最も安全な場所だと思い、「井沢さん！ここは安全だ、壁も貯水槽もある。私が何かあなたを運ぶものを探して来るまでここで待ったほうがいい。」と伝えると彼女はうなずいた。井沢さんにこんなことを言うのは非情だったとも思えるかもしれないが、危険に囲まれた状況でそう言うより仕方がなかった。

　私が彼女から離れた後、彼女は火の手に囲まれて通りすがりの年配女性と共に貯水槽に飛び込み、貯水槽の中で落ち着かない一晩を過ごし、翌日広島通信病院の救助車に発見され救助された後、病院へ運ばれ治療を受けたということ、またその日に彼女の父親は亡くなり母親は重傷を負ったということを、後に伝え聞いた。その彼女も今は回復し、母親と同居しながら広島のとある印刷会社で事務員として働いている。原子爆弾投下の第1回記念日に、彼女は私に話しかけてきて一包みのお米をお礼にと頂いた。それがなんと幸せな出会いであったことか！

　彼女から離れた後、私は橋の方に向かって走り始めた。その路上で私は上司の間島さんが奥さんに付き添われて路上に横たわっているのを再び見つけ、奥さんは私に「尾崎さん！来て私の夫を助けてください！」と叫んだ。幸運にも私は伊達さん（後に彼は死んでしまった）が走っているのを見た。私は彼に呼び掛け上司を助けるように頼んだ。伊達さんの同意を得て私は近くの倒壊した家から板を持って来て上司を板の上に乗せ、我々は彼を運び始めた。1区画ほど歩いた後、我々は広々とした庭のある倒壊した家を見つけた。我々はここがつかの間の避難所になるだろうと思い門を入り、庭の一角に彼を降ろした。この時には火の手が2方向から上がっていた。そこで私は伊達さんと共に上司と奥さんに別れを告げた。

　その後間島さんはどうなったのであろうか？2日後に私が彼らと別れた場所に行った時には、私は彼も彼の遺骸品も見なかった。おそらく救助隊が彼をどこかほかの場所に埋めるために運んだのであろう。彼の奥さんは、後に彼女から説明をうけたところによると、我々が彼らから離れて5分後に間島さんは息を引き取り、たまたま通りかかった地方長の娘と一緒に川へ、それから警察へ、そこから東練兵場へと向かった。そこで落ち着かない2晩を過ごした後、彼女は市の西部にある親友の元へ向かった。彼女はかの有名な能楽師金剛巌（こんごういわお）の娘である。

　私は上司と奥さんと別れた後、苦労をして橋までたどり着いたものの、橋の向こう側の家並み全てが燃え盛っていて橋を渡ることができなかった。そして私の背後からも火の手が上がり、私は浅瀬の砂の上に飛び降りた。その拍子に手に持っていた私のリュックサックが川に落ち水に浮かんでしまった！はじめ私はリュックサックを取り戻すのをあきらめようかと思った。しかしあのリュックサックの中身はこの広い世界で私の持

つ全てのものであった。銀行通帳、いくつかの洋服、わずかな食糧、それにその他の重要な持ち物が入っている、そのため私は考え直し水に飛び込み、3分ほど泳いだ後に水に浮かぶリュックサックを捕まえた。

　　私は砂の上に座り何をすべきか考えたが、何のいい考えも計画も頭に浮かばなかった。橋の下に200人ほどの避難者が群れをなして砂の上にいるのを見た。彼らのほとんどは血まみれの服をまとい、特に顔に重傷を負い、裸足で何の持ち物もバッグも持っていなかった。そこに全部で5人位の軍隊が軍旗を掲げてやって来た。彼らの内のある中尉は手に流血の重傷を負っていて、私に彼の手を縛るようにと頼んだ。私は包帯になるものを持っていなかったので、自分の白いTシャツを割いて流血する手を縛った。彼はとても感謝してくれた。しばらくした後、彼ら軍隊は小さなボートを見つけ軍旗を掲げながら川上を漕いで行った。橋の向こう側の炎が強風に吹かれ梁のかけらが川のこちら側まで吹き飛ばされてきた。とても危険だったのでそれを避けるために我々は頻繁に川に飛び込んだ。その日朝食を摂っていなかったので、この時点では私はとてもお腹が空いていた。私は水流に浮かぶ玉葱のかけらを見つけ泳いで行って取り、リュックサックの中に見つけた米つぶと一緒に食べた。緊急時にはどんな食べ物でも空腹を満たすことができることを実感した。

　　朝の10時ごろには、黒雲と共に雨がみじめな避難者の顔に降り注ぎ始めた。この時私はひっきりなしに続く巨大な爆撃音を聞いた。その場にいた人々はその爆撃音が飛行機からの攻撃ではないかと恐れ、狭い場所をそこここへと走り廻った。しかしすぐにその爆撃音はどこかの弾薬庫が爆発しているという情報が入った。この時までには炎は四方八方にあった。私は自分の人生の終わりを思いとても寂しい気持ちになった。しかし幸運なことに、川の水は段々と引いてゆき、より広い砂面が現れた。400メートル程向こうに行けば、東警察署があることを知っていた、私はその避難所に行き緊急援助を受けるつもりであった。そこで私は浅瀬の砂を歩き始めた。

第2章

丘を越えて

「ひとつの門が閉じるとき、ひとつの窓が開く」

—イタリアの

私は砂の上を時々飛びながら歩いた。街の至る所で起こった炎はその日一日中燃え続け、ギラギラ光る熱と煙が大地と空の全てを覆った。私は火事によって倒壊した家が割れる音を聞いた。木々は燃え盛り空の中で電流のような火花を散らして壊れた。私は市の向こう側にある丘から煙が出ているのを見た。真夏の日差しが残酷にもみじめな人々の頭上を照りつけた。私は砂の上に多くの避難者が重傷を負い意気消沈し、親友や友人から助けられ、傷口を布切れで縛っているのを見た。母親の腕に抱かれた赤ちゃんが死のうとしていた。彼らのこれから来るであろう災難を期待する表情は悲惨で絶望的であった。どこに行けるというのだろうか?いなくなった人々、叔母たち、兄弟に姉妹、愛する者たちは今どこにいるというのであろうか?迫り来る昼と夜の食べ物はどのように供給されるというのであろうか?

「私には安らぎもなく、休みもなく、いこいもなく、心はかき乱されている。」（ヨブ記第3章26節）私は聖書のヨブ記を引用して文句を言わずにはいられなかった。

私は川の砂から土手へとよじ登った。あちこちでたくさんの死体を見た。男性、女性、年配者に若者、子供に赤ん坊、それに猫や犬まで、顔の半分が焼けている者や、ガラスの破片によって切り傷を負い裸の者や、煙と炎によって真黒になっている者。私はそのような悲惨な姿を見る我慢ができなかった。燃え続ける家の煙に混じった死体の臭いが通りに充満していた。

私は浅瀬の小高い所に立ち、辺りを見回した。火事に次ぐ火事、倒壊に次ぐ倒壊であった。愛すべき我々の都市広島が燃えていた！我々の愛しい住居は終末を迎えようとしていた。すべて消え去った。西にも東にも炎が上がり、広島はすでに無くなっていた。どの方向からも焼けるような暑さを感じた。市民は死に、埋められ、家は倒壊し、路面電車や自動車は燃えていた！私が立つ場所の西側で、高層コンクリート建ての中国新聞ビルと巨大な福屋デパートの窓から容赦なく炎の手が押し出るのを見た。かつて日曜礼拝に通ったメソジスト教会の高いほうのタワーの十字架から煙が出ていた。コンクリート建ての建物のみが、中にある家具や他の物はみな燃えて灰と化したものの、骨組みや構造が残っていた。私は我々のラジオ局はコンクリート建てなので、中が燃えたとしても残るだろうと知った。

　やっとのことで広島東駅にたどり着いたものの、何人かの重傷を負った警察官が部屋に横たわっていて、営業している事務所はひとつも無かった。部屋の角で壊れた給水管から新鮮な水が噴き出しているのを見つけて、がぶがぶ飲んだ。夏の日差しと熱から来る喉の渇きにはその水はとても甘く、私はコップ数杯分を飲んだ。事務所の近くにそのうち燃えてなくなりそうな自転車が何台かあった。誰も聞く人がいなかったので、この緊急事態に無許可で自転車を借りることを決めた。神よ、許したまえ！危険と炎から逃げるために必要だった。そして私は自転車に乗り、何度も燃え続ける通りを抜け、何度も煙立つ橋を渡り、市の東側へと向かった。

　数多くの困難の後、ついに東練兵場にたどり着いた。そこで私は避難者が苦難の後疲れ果て、重傷を負い、ほとんど裸で何の持ち物も持たずに、あちこちで集団になり乾いた地面で休んでいるのを見た。人々はひどく重傷を負った人々を背負ったり板に乗せたりして運んでいた。

　私は芝生に横たわり、空を見上げ、新鮮な空気の中で深呼吸した。燃え続ける都市の煙を吸い続けていただけに、空気はとても新鮮に感じた。ひどい疲労感を感じ、今なにをすれば良いのだろう？と考えていた。私は、もし我々の放送局（スタジオ）が何らかの悲劇的な状況で破壊された場合、我々は退去してそこから3キロ程北に向かった所にある原放送局に集合するように伝えられていたことを思い出した。しかしそこに直接向かう横川通りを抜ける道は、炎に閉ざされていた。そこで私はまずここから原村の東側を廻って丘を過ぎ、川を渡って目的地の原放送局に行こうと決断した。

　そう決断すると、私は心の中に少しの希望が生まれるのを感じた。私が横たわるこの場所は広島の東側の郊外にあった。すぐそばの家並みは市街から遠いにも関わらず、何軒かの家は焼けていて、屋根全部や窓ガラス、家の弱くなった部分は吹き飛ばされ、何軒かの家は強い爆破により半倒壊状態になっていた。重傷を負った人々はあちこちで助けを求めながら、あてもなくさまよっていた。重傷を負っていない人は数少なかった。私は自分が安全であったことを神に感謝した。

　私は30分間の休憩の後で、再び自転車に乗り丘の上へと向かった。あれは午後2時ごろであった。空腹を感じた。自転車に乗った路上で、たまたまある家を見かけた。私は誰が住んでいるかも知らずに不意に門の中へと入った。中年の女性と女の子がいた。また、どの部屋にもたくさんの避難者がいた。私が燃え続ける市内から逃げてきたこと、しばらく休憩がしたいことを説明すると、彼らは私を部屋に入れてくれ、親切にもお菓子とお茶を出してくれた。リュックサックに少しのお米が入っていたので、私は女性からもらったじゃがいもと一緒に自分で料理をした。昼食を食べた後私は彼らに別れを告げ自転車で丘へ向かった。途中で、軍のトラックがたくさんの重傷を負った人々を荷台に乗せ、丘の道を北区へと突進しているのを見た。その避難者達ほとんど裸で、顔や髪は焼けて、何人かは血まみれの服をまとっていたため、男女の区別はできなかった。

　私の背後に一台の車がゆっくりと来た。車内に目をやると身分の高そうな軍の将校が重傷を負った顔を包帯で巻かれ横たわっているのを見た。後に私は、彼が軍役に服していた韓国の王子で、あの日原子爆弾の爆心地相生橋近く馬に乗っていたところで重傷を負い、彼の副官は彼の近くにいなかったという責任感にさいなまれ自殺したということを聞いた。途中には小学校があった。たくさんの避難者がそこに集まっており、負傷者は医療手当を受け、乾パンまたはお米の配給を受けていた。この時丘の坂は急になりつつあり、私は自転車を降りて歩き始めた。負傷者で荷台がいっぱいになったトラックが突進し、そこから私の名前を呼ぶ女性の声が聞こえた。

　「尾崎さん！尾崎さん！」

「どなたですか？」私は不思議に思った

「山崎です、ラジオ局の事務員の……背中にひどい重傷を負ってしまいました。」彼女は言った。

彼女は2枚の簡素な切れ端をまとい悲しい表情で車の中ほどに座っていた。

「あなたでしたか！体に気をつけて！神が救いたまうでしょう！あなたのことは部長にちゃんと伝えておきます。少し待ってくださいね。」

トラックは通り過ぎ姿を消した。彼女に関して言えば、その後治療を受け回復し現在は私達の局で働いている。

私は途中で私達の局で働く2人の事務の女性に会った。一人は足に重傷を負い、杖をついて歩いていた。私は彼女達がどうやって放送局からここまで来たかを尋ねた。彼女達はまず川まで走り、近くに浮かんでいた船で川を渡り、ここまで牛田山を越えて来たとのことであった。私は彼女達に祝いの言葉を述べた。村の近くの友人宅に行くということで、私は彼女達と別れた。

一時間ほど後に私は川にたどり着き、渡らなければならなかった。渡し船があり、男の子が漕いでいた。彼は私と自転車をその船に乗せてくれた。川の向こう岸に着いた後、わたしは運賃がいくらかを聞いた。

「運賃？僕が避難者からお金を取れると思うのですか？見た感じ、広島から来たのでしょう、避難者からお金を取るどころかむしろ助けなければならないでしょう。」

私はとても感動し目頭が熱くなるのを感じた。彼は、この国の仲間達が災害に苦しんでいることを知っていたのだ！

私は土手へと来た。夕暮れ時であった。そこにいた村人に原放送局への道を聞くと、自転車で20分ほどの道のりだと言われた。1台のトラックが荷台に食糧や配給品を載せて広島の方向に突進していた。そのトラックが私の側を通り過ぎたとき、トラックにいた誰かが何か投げた。その何かが乾パンだとわかり、私は天国からの贈り物かのように彼らに感謝した。午後6時半に私は安全に局にたどり着いた。すでに10人ほどの同僚が市内からたどり着いていて、残りの同僚が到着するのを待っていた。惨禍に見舞われ、皆途方に暮れていた。部長はそこにいて、私は自分のすべての経験を細かく説明した。局にいた友人は私を歓迎しタオルや他の物をくれ、ご飯とみそ汁をくれた。

爆破により事務所の窓ガラスや屋根が壊れており、私はこの原放送局が広島から5キロほど離れているにも関わらず、何らかの原子爆弾の被害を受けていることに気がついた。原子爆弾の影響がどれだけ大きいのかを理解した。この局には事務所の周りに広い庭がある。私は庭に出た。暗闇の中私は庭のあちこちでクローバーの花が咲き誇ろうとしているのを見た。静寂であった。しかし5キロほど向こうの南の空で、巨大な炎がまるで昼間のように明るく市街を覆い激しく燃え盛っていた。

広島が！愛する都市、我が家が！私は芝生にひざまずき、我が家にいた母、市の近くの工場で働いていた一人息子の誠一（せいいち）、それにその時点で安否が定かでなかった友人や彼らの家族の安全を神に祈った。これは広島の終わりなのであろうか？それに私の人生の終わりであろうか？私は祈った。神は私を救ってくれていると感じた。この悲劇と不運にも関わらず、神は私の傍にいた。このような災難の中でも、日本にはまだ住める場所も避難する場所もある。災難は私を強くしてくれた。私は聖書の一節を思い出した。

「それだけではなく、患難をも喜んでいる。なぜなら、患難は忍耐を生み出し、忍耐は錬達を生み出し、錬達は希望を生み出すことを、知っているからである。」（ローマの信徒への手紙5章3節）

　そうだ！錬達と希望だ！冷たい風が私を瞑想から起こしてくれた。私は中に入り、硬い床の上に毛布で寝る準備をした。しかし私は少しも眠れず、心も体も落ち着かないまま夜を過ごした。

第3章

愛する者を探して

「明らかに、環境や状況そのものが私たちを幸せにしたり不幸せにしたりするわけではない。私達の感情は、私達がその状況にどう反応するかによって決定される。私達は皆災害を耐え抜くことができるし、勝利を収めることもできる、必要とあらば。私達は自分達が思っているよりも強靭である。」

—デール・カーネギー

私は重いまぶたを開けた。体がだるかった。通常時、人は正常に動くことができる。しかし緊急事態において、状況に応じて正常に物事を行うのは難しくなる。そして人々が災害に面して途方に暮れているとき、災害に対して何か行動を起こすことはできなくなる。朝の冷たい風に吹かれ私達は我に返り、まず何をしなければならないか、という考えが皆の頭に浮かんだ。朝第一にしなければならなかったことは、東京ラジオ放送局に我々の緊急事態を報告することであった。ほとんどの中継線や発信線は爆破により切断されていたが、広島から姫路市経由で東京に接続する線が1本残っているのを発見した。そこで我々は「飛行機の攻撃により市街は崩壊し、我々の放送局は火事となり、たくさんの同僚が死亡し、破壊的な損害を受け…等々」短い報告を送信した。我々の放送局でやるべきことはたくさんあった。しかし前述のように、全ての中継線と発信線は破壊されていたため、次にやる事として、近隣と東京の放送局からの支援を待つ間に行方不明の同僚や家族を探す事に決めた。

　そのため、私は放送局を去り自転車に乗り家族を捜すために広島へ向かった。広島への道は市へ向かう人や市から来る人々で混みあっていた。重傷を負った人々、重いリュックサックを背負った人々、車、荷車、避難者と物がいっぱいに載ったトラック。何人かは起こった出来事に興奮し、何人かは疲労にうなだれ、夏の灼熱のため自転車に乗るのも大変であった。私は市の入り口にあたる横川に来た。食糧と配給品をいっぱいに載せたトラックがあり、誰かが私に声をかけ米の配給をくれた。そこからは自転車に乗り続けることが更に難しくなった。たくさんの電柱や、倒壊した家、たくさんの梁に割れた石等が道をふさぎ、橋は落ちて燃えていたからである。そのため私はいつも通る道を通って我が家へ直接帰ることはできなかった。私は何度も進路を変え、時々煙立つ橋を渡りながら、回り道をしなければならなかった。私は頻繁に躓いたが、なんとしても、我が家の近くの西の橋に行かなければならなかった。私は路上に、そして川に、た

くさんの死体を見た。途中で広島中央電話局西分局の近くにある防空壕からかすかな声が聞こえてきた。中をのぞくと、数人の女の子が裸で全身にやけどを負い、ひどい重体でお互いに抱き合っているのを見つけた。わずかに動いていたものの、彼女達のほとんどは今にも息を引き取りそうに見えた。一人の女の子がとてもか細い声で「お母さん！お母さん！」と呼んでいる声が聞こえた。私は彼女に名前を尋ねたが返事は無かった。彼女達を救う手段が無かったので、私は彼女たちを助けることができなかった。そのため、私は目を閉じ彼女達のために祈った。近くには一人の女性が、腕に赤ちゃんを抱えて、目にいっぱいの涙をためて歩いていた。私はその赤ちゃんがすでに死んでいるのだとわかった。

　ついに私は橋の近くの我が家にたどり着き、家が燃えて灰になっているのを発見した。人生で最悪な経験であった。もしかしたら下から母の遺骸が出てくるのではないかと恐れながら、私が灰や割れた石、金属などを手で押しのけている時、背後から声が聞こえた。

　　「おばあちゃんは無事だよ。」

　声を聞いてとても驚いた。その声の主は息子で、無事であった。我々は泣いて抱き合い、神に感謝した。息子の説明によると、工場で爆発音が聞こえた後、彼は爆風により倒されたものの、傷は負わなかった。彼は急いで工場から20分ほどの家に駆け戻った。家にたどり着いたとき、我が家は燃えており祖母は近所の人と門の所に立っていた。彼は荷車を見つけ、祖母と近所の人をその上に載せ、橋を渡って一番近くの村へと逃げ始めた。荷車をひいて20分ほどした時、後援のトラックがたまたま通りすがり、彼らを10キロほど離れたところにある漁村の地御前へと運んでくれた。現在は小学校の避難所に住んでいる、ということだった。

　私は息子の知らせを聞いてとても嬉しく思った。そしてすぐにそこへ母に会いに行くことに決めた。地御前に徒歩で着くころには夕方であった。学校のバラックは避難者で混み合っていた。私は母が運動場の角のマットの上で、若干興奮した様子で左足をけがして休んでいるのを見つけた。母は私の安全を知ってとても喜んだ。

　ご飯とみそ汁が配られ、服やシャツも配給された。学校の校舎内の部屋は混み合っていて幾人かは死につつあった。そのため私達は運動場で夜を過ごすことに決めた。しかし、その日起こった出来事から来る興奮と、蚊に邪魔されて眠ることができなかった。

第4章

焼けた市街

「人は困難から学ぶ。」

— パスカル

8月8日は輝く朝日と共に来た。私は母と息子の世話を責任者に頼み別れを告げた。放送局でしなければならないことがたくさんあったからである。

　私は市の中心へと来た。なんということか！砂漠であった！人々は今この地を原爆砂漠と呼んでいる。居住者も木も無く、事実生きているものは何も無く、路面電車はあちこちで焼け焦げて止まっていた。死の匂いが通りに漂っていた。市の中心近くにある頑強な鉄筋コンクリートでできた相生橋は、いくつかの部分が壊れていた。厚い鉄筋金属は曲がり、橋の壁は爆破されていた。私は広島郵便局の従業員200名ほどが生き埋めになりその場で即死したということ、2、3名のみが救助されたこと、そして広島県庁の従業員600名ほどが同じ運命をたどったということを聞いた。たまたま市の中心近くを走っていた路面電車の全ての乗客は、あの日あの瞬間に一瞬にして死んでしまった！歴史上、莫大な規模の犠牲である。

　私は福屋デパートの前に来た。派手な電灯や店員達の陽気なおしゃべりの声はもう無い。煙を立て燃えながら、コンクリートの外壁と床だけが残っていた。私はかつて勧業銀行があった交差点に来た。たくさんの重傷を負った市民が銀行の床に横たわっていた。彼らのほとんどは顔の皮膚が焼けただれ、皆泣き叫んでいた。何人かの医者や看護婦が傷に包帯を巻いたり注射を打ったりして彼らを治療していた。

　ついに私はラジオ局にたどり着いた。背後にあった新しい木造の事務所はもう無かったが、本社ビルは残っていた。私はそこへ正面口から入った。全ての放送機器とキャビネットは破壊され、家具や、本、レコードは全て焼けて灰になっていた。給水設備の水道管が切断されそこから水が噴出して部屋を水でいっぱいにしていた。私は企画部の部屋に入った。金属以外は全て灰に変わっていた。部屋は以前に比べかつてないほど広くなったように見えた。私は火事の以前に持っていた飯盒を見つけ、記念に持って帰ることにした。次に私は防空壕に入り全ての個人のおよび職務上の貴重品が燃えてくずでいっぱいになっているのを見つけた。私は放送局の屋上に上り辺りを見回した。コンクリートの建物と半焼の木以外は何も残っていない、砂漠だった。比治山がとても近くに見えた。

　原放送局に行く途中、私は練兵場があった広島城跡を見に行った。そこには城も軍隊のバラックも無かった。私は古い城跡付近の堀や練兵場の敷地内に、たくさんの兵隊

の死体が横たわっているのを見た。半焼の木々や城跡の石、遺骸品は兵隊達の過去の輝かしい日々の夢を物語っていた。軍国主義と封建主義は消えてしまった。私は焼け野原をさまよい歩き、過去の日々を思い出していた。

　夕方私は原放送局へと戻った。我々は従業員のために放送局近くの農家の部屋を借りることにした。放送局の同僚のうち35名ほどが亡くなったものの、企画部の事務員が全員無事だったのは幸運だった。数名のみが軽傷を負い、妻や子を亡くした。

　広島に落ちた巨大な爆弾については前述のようにたくさんの噂があった。日本のG.H.Q（連合国軍最高司令官総司令部）は巨大で強力な化学爆弾が投下され市民と住居に莫大な惨禍をもたらしたという簡単な声明を出した。後に我々はアメリカの情報により、あの惨禍をもたらしたのは原子爆弾そのものであったということを告げられ、更にほとんどの死亡被害や負傷は放射能によるものだったと初めて理解した。

　広島とその郊外には今後75年間は人も木もどんな生きる物も生きることができないという噂が広まった。そこで市内の倒壊した家や防空壕に残った避難者達は国内の別な場所へと避難し始めた。実を言うと、市民の死亡率は上がっていた。放射能を受けた市民は髪が抜け始め、肌にシミが浮かび、死んでいった。何人もが血液中の放射能により死んでいった。全ての火葬場は破壊されたので、遺族は自分たちで最愛の家族を焼かなければならなかった。

　広島の出来事から数日たって、世界最大の出来事は2つ目の原爆が長崎に投下されたことと、ロシア軍の満州侵攻によるロシアの日本に対する宣戦布告であった。不幸は不幸を呼ぶものだ。

　我々はどうやってそのような攻撃を持ちこたえられようか？日本の終わりが近づこうとしていた。陸軍も海軍もなんの力も残っていなかった。

　この頃には、日本は連合軍との和平交渉を行っているという情報があった。後に我々は8月15日の正午ちょうどに天皇陛下から何か厳粛な声明が発表されるとのことで、その時間帯全ての車両および乗り物は声明を聞くために運行停止という命令が出された。我々はその速報を放送するためにとても忙しかった。国民は皆心配しながら待ちきれなさそうにこの瞬間を待った。

　あの日、全ての乗り物も通りの人々も立ち止まり、家庭や会社にいた人々も熱心にラジオを聞いた。最初に東京のアナウンサーが紹介され、そして天皇陛下の声を聞き、終戦の日が来たことを知った！しかし無条件降伏であった。私はあの歴史的瞬間の印象をペンで表現することができない。我々国民がどのように感じ、この国に今後何が起こるのであろうかということを。全ての人がそれぞれ複雑な思いを抱いてすすり泣いた。全ての兵隊は解放され海外から帰国し始めた。戦争中に都市から農村へと疎開していた人々はそれぞれの家や彼らの焼けた都市へと帰る準備をし、全ての鉄道路線や船や車は、このような大きなリュックサックを背負った人々で混雑した。連合国がこの地にたどり着くまで、車両や路上の混雑がしばらく続いた。

　私の個人的な事を言うならば、市内に戻り半倒壊の我が家に居た母は、9月1日の早朝足の重傷が原因で死んでしまった。私は息子と共に母の体に油をかけ、火を付けた！そんな事をするのは残酷に思われるかもしれない、しかしあの緊急事態においては仕方がなかったことは、神のみぞ知る。巨大な洪水が9月17日の真夜中に起きた時、私は母の遺骸を埋めるために瀬戸内海を渡って生まれ故郷の四国へと行く準備をしていた。数日間雨が降り続いていた。午前零時、私は誰かが「洪水！洪水！」と叫んでいる声に起こされた。私は窓を開けた。なんということか！水深は我々が住む小さな家の2階まで来ていた。もし家が瓦礫と共に水に流されてしまったら、どうなるのだろうか？私は容赦なく流れる水の中に丸太や倒壊した家を見た。我々には避難する手段が無かったた

め、夜が明けることと水が引くのを待つのみであった。幸い朝が近づくにつれて水深は
浅くなっていった。

　そして夜明けには我々は安全だと感じていた。水深は60センチほどに下がってい
た。火事の後に洪水！この洪水の被害により農作物や野菜の収穫が減少するであろうと
いう発表があった。我は憂鬱になった。私は母の遺骸を抱き、あの洪水の日の午後、私
は息子と共に思い切って6キロ程南に離れた港へ向かった。

　洪水の波を何度も渡り道のりは困難であった。市内に来た時は夜であった。辺りは
暗く居住者もいない「死の街」であった。我々は壊れた路面電車を見つけ2時間ほど休
憩のために中で過ごし、また港へと出発した。翌朝早く我々は母の遺骸を埋めるため、
私の生まれ故郷へ行く船に乗った。

　その年秋のある明るい日に、占領軍の兵隊が旧海軍港である呉に到着した。新しい
日が来た！

第5章

平和の到来

「我々は日本国民が民族として奴隷化もしくは国家として滅亡す
ることを意図しない。日本政府は日本国民が復興する上での全て
障害を取り除き、民主化の傾向を強化する。」

― ポツダム宣言より

最初の原子爆弾が広島の地に投下されたあの忘れがたき日から4年の月日がたった。戦争が無くなった日本では民主主義国としての一歩を踏み出した。全てが変わった！封建的な日本は消えた！1947年11月3日新しい日本国憲法が公布された。そして「言論の自由、宗教の自由、思想の自由、基本的人権の尊重」が確立された。兵隊は解放された。全て海外の兵隊は、中国、シベリア、南海方面から焼けて倒壊した故郷へと帰って来た。陸軍と海軍は完全に武器を放棄し、日本国領土は日本列島に限定され多くの殖民地を失った。結果として、戦後のこの国の人口は近い将来この狭い領域内で八千万人になろうとしていた。一方で、政治的及び社会的状況はしばらくの間混乱していた。

インフレの影響で日々の生活は日に日に苦しくなり、至る所に闇市が増えた。家や食べ物、衣服は過少になり価格は日に日に上昇した。泥棒、強盗犯、殺人犯が警察署の部屋をいっぱいにした。落ち着かない日々と気の休めない夜が長く続いた。特に軍隊教育と訓練を受けた若者たちは人生の目標を失ったかのように見えた。そして彼らは民主主義の真の意味を誤解し、生き方は粗雑で無秩序となり、通りや闇市でさまよい歩くか、集団になって犯罪を犯した。

本屋には安く不道徳な本や雑誌、印刷物が売られていた。主婦たちは農家に行き貴重な着物と交換にお米やとうもろこし、野菜を買って来た。

事実上、日本は混乱のるつぼの中にいた。しかし終戦3年目の後半から、社会的状況はある程度良くなり、連合国軍（特にアメリカとイギリスが）食糧、衣服、その他の物に手を広げアンラ（UNRRA連合国救済復興機関）やララ（LARAアジア救済公認団体）の救援物資は孤児や未亡人や家を無くした人々を活気づけた。食糧は増加し、衣服は配給され、家屋は建設された。

希望と復興！我々は惨禍にも関わらず国民のための新計画を実行しなければならない。広島においては、現在245,000人の居住者がいる（原子爆弾以前は312,200人であった）。そして住居は60,000件（原子爆弾以前は76,000件)となり、デパート、銀行、映画館ができ、公務員の人も会社勤めの人も皆仕事を始めた。路面電車は運行し始め、暖かい喫茶店やきれいなカフェやレストランも営業を開始した。

　海外から貨物でいっぱいの船が宇品港に着き、外国人は原子爆弾の被害はどのようなものかと毎日原爆投下跡地を見にやって来た。広島は復興しつつあった。「ノーモア・ヒロシマ」のキャンペーンは日本国内でも世界中でも活発的になっている。

　現在我々は、新しい日本国憲法が平和を愛する人々に宣言するように、喜びと希望をもって声高らかに「日本国民は、国権の発動たる戦争と、武力による威嚇又は武力の行使は、国際紛争を解決する手段としてはこれを永久に放棄する」。つまり、あの日は決して広島の最後の日ではなく、新たな始まりの日だったのだ。

― 完 ―

广岛之歌

广岛之歌

序

诺埃尔·卡彭

1999年，94岁的洛伊斯·克鲁斯（Lois Crews）在纽约长岛的华盛顿港逝世。因为我和妻子迪安娜（Deanna）是她的近亲，所以由我们查看她的财产，决定保留些什么，并准备好拍卖她的房子。在检查阁楼时，我无意中发现了一个好像孩子用的笔记本，上面记录了些什么。几个星期后，我看了这本笔记。现在，这本《广岛之歌》由韦塞克斯（Wessex）出版。

　　第二次世界大战之前，洛伊斯（Lois）的丈夫阿尔伯特·克鲁斯（Albert Crews）在美国国家广播公司（NBC）工作。二战结束后，作为麦克阿瑟将军（General MacArthur）的幕僚之一，他在广岛工作了几个星期，指导过广播电台的工作。阿尔伯特（Albert）从负责通信和翻译的干事尾崎淳博（Atsuhiro Ozaki）那里得到了这本手写的笔记。

　　1945年8月6日，尾崎（Ozaki）先生正在广播电台上班，那里距原子弹降落点不到一公里。他交给阿尔伯特·乔斯（Albert Crews）的笔记描写了原子弹爆炸后的两三天内他的所见所闻和亲身经历。尾崎（Ozaki）先生把笔记交给阿尔伯特·克鲁斯（Albert Crews），是希望能与美国人民分享自己的经历。我们不知道阿尔伯特（Albert）是否曾经使用过这份材料，也不知道这本笔记是否就在华盛顿港的阁楼里放了半个多世纪。不管怎样，虽然已经过去了六十年，这本出版物还是实现了尾崎淳博（Atsuhiro Ozaki）的愿望。

　　为了广泛传播这份材料，韦塞克斯（Wessex）正在用英语、日语、西班牙语和汉语出版这本《广岛之歌》。我们还复制了尾崎淳博（Atsuhiro Ozaki）写给阿尔伯特（Albert）的信和他的完整笔记。在出版中，为了帮助读者理解，我们对尾崎（Ozaki）先生原文的拼写略作修改，并进行了简单的编辑。

诺埃尔·卡彭
纽约布朗士维尔
2011年1月1日

诺艾尔 卡彭是纽约哥伦比亚大学商学院R.C.考普夫国际市场营销学教授。迪娜 琨是纽约哥伦比亚大学教育学院教育和心理学教授。

广岛之歌

— 1945年8月6日 —

尾崎淳博

日本·广岛
广岛中央广播电台节目部

前言

"内心没有痛到极处的时代，生活中就没有伟大的音乐。"

—卡尔·巴斯

再过几个月，就是历史上那个难忘时刻的第四个纪念日。那是1945年8月6日，第一颗原子弹落在我们亲爱的广岛土地上和街道上的日子。如今，那里的七条河依然奔流着晶莹的河水。现在正值春天：樱花像往常一样在岸边绽放—那里曾经是我们挚爱亲人散步的地方；云雀依然在空中歌唱；青翠的草木重新从冻土中探出头来。我们挚爱亲人的坟丘上，鲜花开了又谢，谢了又开。大自然没有改变，而人类已经改变。我们曾经挚爱的亲人不复存在，我们曾经拥的老房子连同舒适的房间和昂贵的家具一起消失！不过，上帝有取也有授。虽然经历了这场考验，我们仍有一些人满怀活下去的希望和力量留了下来。

新时代就在那个历史时刻萌生。为了迎接新时代，幸存者"无所畏惧"地从原子弹留下的残垣断壁上站起来。明亮的灯光透过狭窄新棚屋的窗户，照亮了遭焚毁的花园，"广岛重建之歌"的旋律回荡在黑暗的星空。

"让我们重建广岛
天将破晓，我们满心欢喜；
锤声阵阵，在晨风中回荡，
希望升起在'原子荒漠'。"

是的！重建就有希望。

现在，请让我说明为什么要写这个笔记。那个难忘日子的早晨，我正在广岛中央广播电台的办公室上班，那里距第一颗原子弹降落地点不到一公里。原子弹爆炸后，我的同事中约有三十五名遇难，我亲爱的母亲还在我们位于市郊的家里。她受了重伤，后来也去世了。幸运的是我所在的房间围着厚厚的墙壁，我很安全，没有受到丝毫伤害。我失去了亲爱的母亲、我的家、我的家具、我最喜爱的书籍和财产，也失去了我工作过的办公室，那是多么痛苦的经历啊！人类历史上曾经有过瞬间造成如此重大损失的事件记录吗？

那个时候，广岛大约有366,000人。第一颗原子弹爆炸后，辐射和房屋倒塌导致92,133人死亡，9,428人受重伤，27,997人受轻伤；幸存176,987人；8,200幢房屋（该城的90%）被焚为灰烬；因辐射而死亡的人数在逐日增加，由46,185人上升至70,000人。（这些数字中还不包括士兵和服役人员）著名的遗址和珍贵的历史纪念碑及建筑都消失了！一切都消失了！我们挚爱的亲人和所有的一切都在一瞬间消失！

暴风雨一场接着一场。在大约一个月的时间内，日本广岛地区不仅经历了这场灾难，还在 9月17日遭遇一场幽灵般大洪水的袭击，造成巨大的人员和财产损失。（1,199人死去或溺水，897人下落不明，房屋和农村土地也遭受重大损失。）

战争结束后，我曾经和办公室的朋友们讨论，虽然我们的书写能力有限，也不能谈及我们想要做什么，但是我们应该记录下如此可怕的经历和事件，作为资料留给后代。然而，当时我们非常忙，要盖新房子，还要重建自己的生活，恢复广播电台的工作。四年恍若一场梦，一转眼过去了。但是，那不是梦，那是现实——在未来的人类之间将不会再有冲突或战争。

和平已经降临这个长期遭受压迫者和独裁者折磨的封建制国家！新时代真的到来了！而我在那一天亲眼所见，亲耳所听，亲身经历的一切，一定要写进备忘录或日记中。那是我的责任，是对我们国家、对世界上热爱和平人民应尽的责任。

> "我属于日本，
> 日本属于世界，
> 世界属于基督，
> 一切属于上帝"
>
> ——内村鉴三

这确实是一部人类文献，旨在叙述发生在第一颗原子弹降落广岛那天早上发生的生动事件和事实真相。然而，因为自己的英语知识贫乏，我担心不能准确描述我所经历的一切，不过，叙述事实本身就将证明真正发生了什么。有关合乎科学的医学研究，一定会有其他人去做。我的目的只是叙述亲身的经历。

我的职业生涯：自关西学院（由美国传教士兰伯雷斯（Lambreth）博士创建的卫理公会教派大学）毕业后，我曾做过牧师、英语教师、新闻记者，现在是广岛中央广播电台的无线电通信员。现在，我住在"原子荒漠"一个简陋的小屋里，以普通人的身份享受着新日本的日常生活。

尾崎淳博
1949年5月

第一章

那一天

"磨难在增强基督徒的快乐。"

—皮克

那确实是1945年8月6日，天气依然晴朗而炎热。自1944年下半年起，美国飞机日复一日，夜复一夜的空袭将最重要的目标和城市炸得粉碎或焚为灰烬，东京及其市郊已经遭到几次袭击，损伤惨重。美国占领马里亚纳群岛后，B-29飞机从那里来去自如地袭击我们的城市和重要目标。1945年1月3日，90架飞机飞抵名古屋；台湾和冲绳遭受攻击，受到500架舰载飞机的轰炸；1月30日，美国陆军和海军冒险登陆马尼拉湾；2月16日，美国特遣部队登陆Iwo-shima岛，在那里展开了历史上最惨烈的战斗；3月13日和17日，大阪和神户分别经受大规模攻击和火灾的破坏；3月21日，在双方都损失了许多条生命和许多枪支之后，美国特遣部队终于占领Iwo-shima岛。这个时候，大多数重要城市和这些岛上的基地都遭到B-29或舰载飞机的攻击；房屋和重要目标被焚毁；人们失去了家园、衣物或食品，不得不四处游荡。这只迷途的羔羊能去哪里？日本面临末日——死亡，处于极度痛苦之中。

纷至沓来的报告和新闻令我们心情忧郁，我们渐渐意识到即将到来的悲惨命运和苦难岁月。政府领导人努力让人们相信最终的胜利，但是他们的呐喊徒劳无功。

这时，从早上起，天气就非常炎热。我在广播电台负责防空通信，接收来自广岛和吴市陆军和海军基地有关敌机行踪的消息。我把收到的大致内容匆匆撰写好，将手稿交给焦急等在我身旁的播音员，由他播发出去。这些工作持续进行了大约两年。我们从早忙到晚，根本没有时间休息，总是神经紧张地接听电话。

那天凌晨两点，空袭警报响起来，当时有两三架飞机飞到广岛市区上空。虽然敌机仍在广岛附近徘徊，但是大约在六点，由于军事基地负责军官的误解，警报解除了。头天晚上逃离广岛市和已经进入防空洞的市民回家了。他们在吃早饭，或准备去办公室、工厂上班。其中有些人已经上街或进了花园，因为前一天晚上经历了恐惧和疲劳，他们要在清晨的微风中重新振作精神。按照日本以往的风俗，在炎热的夏季，那些呆在家里的男人和男孩通常光着身子，什么都不穿，或只穿日本浴衣（一种简单的夏装）或短裤。

就在时钟指向早上8点15分的那一刻，历史上第一颗原子弹落在广岛的土地上！爆炸中心就在爱岐桥（Aigi Bridge）附近，几乎就在市中心。我很幸运，来自军事基地的电话大声响起时（大约早上8点），我和另外两名播音员冲进防空通信室接收情报。就在填完新闻表格，递给负责的播音员时，我听到一声巨响和人们尖利的呼救声，与此同时，天花

板的粉沫落到我的头上。我还看到一连串电石气光般的蓝光涌进来，弥漫了整个房间。我以为我们电台受到了直接的打击。

我抓起椅子座垫捂住头，吓得发抖，不知道这个世界会变成什么样子。我冲进节目部。天哪！房间已经变了样！简直没有插脚的地方，桌椅和其它家具大都损坏，窗玻璃也被震碎，落了下来。我的一些同事倒在地上。他们的脸部和身体被严重炸伤。血从他们的脸上和手上不断涌出。有个人尖叫着求救，因为他的眼睛被炸飞的玻璃片划伤。在这场灾难之中，我不知所措。Dōmei Tsūshinsha（战前有名的日本新闻机构）的一位新闻记者光着身子奔向我，请我给他点东西遮体。碰巧旁边有一件卡其布制服，我递给他，赶紧奔到我的办公桌旁。很幸运，我找到了帽子、西服和装有应急用私人物品的帆布背包。

过了一会，办公室所有的工作人员顾不得头上、手上或脚上的伤，都开始收拾自己的衣物和私人物品，准备逃跑。其中有些人已经逃走，去找更安全的地方。广播电台的某个角落着了火，人们很快用水管扑灭了。

我从破碎的窗户往外看去，哎呀！在我视线之内的所有木质房屋都被炸塌或被炸成碎片，烟、火已经从某些地方冒出来。我很想知道究竟发生了什么事。我看到，广播电台前面的街道上有许多受了重伤的市民。他们几乎光着身子或只穿着衬衫或短裤，正成群结队或独自跑向城市北部。熟人或朋友们在帮助或亲手抬着受重伤的男女，以及痛苦不堪的孩子们。我看到血从他们的脸上、手上还有胸部涌出来。孩子们徒劳地呼喊着失散的父母和兄弟姐妹的名字。有些人赤裸着受伤的身子在街上奔跑。看到市民在这场灾难中遭受那么痛苦的折磨，我不禁想起但丁在《神曲·地狱》（我年轻时看过）中描述的那些可怕细节和情景。

我意识到整个城市都被摧毁了，但是不明白，为什么我们在一瞬间就处于如此可怕而悲惨的境地。这真是不可思议的事情。但是，在那危急的时刻，没有人知道真相，只能含糊地得出这样的结论：一颗威力巨大的巨型炸弹落在地上，或者某种特殊的电力通过某种科学的手段控制了这座城市及其郊区。

不管怎样，在这场灾难中，我自己清醒过来，并设法冲出这个危险地区，去找另一处更安全的避难所。我首先想到生病的母亲和在工厂上班的唯一儿子，可是，大火已经在那个地区烧起来，我无法回到那里。也许上帝会保护他们！于是，我打算跑过离电台最近的荣桥（Sakae Bridge），到"东训练场"去。作出决定后，我赶紧做好准备，穿上西服，背上帆布背包。在下楼的路上，我发现女播音员伊泽小姐（Izawa）躺在地上。她的脚受伤了，无法走路。在朋友们的帮助下，我把她背到大门口，在那里我看到节目部副主任真岛（Majima）先生。他血肉模糊地躺在地上呼救，有些人围着他。

这时，有个女孩拉住我的手，求我救救她父亲。她父亲被压在木材下面，动弹不得，与此同时还有几位朋友在呼救。一个大约两岁的孩子哭喊着在大门附近寻找她失散的妈妈。我茫然不知所措，最后决定先帮助女播音员和我们副主任。我幸运地在大门附近找到一辆婴儿车。在朋友们的帮助下，我在车上放了一块木板，想让他们躺上去。可是，他们太重，立刻把车压碎了，结果两名伤员都掉在地上。于是，我把副主任交给朋友们照顾，同时决心背起伊泽小姐（Izawa）。她那么重，夏季的阳光又那么炎热，路上还到处散落着木板、木棍、碎石，背上她非常困难。

我背着伊泽小姐（Izawa），一路上摔倒了两三次，跌跌撞撞地走了大约两个街区。那个时候，几乎没有人在逃跑，而且附近几个地方着了火。我们在一幢宅邸大门前停下来。这座宅邸属于中国区（Chugoku）的行政署长Awaya先生。我发现宅邸的墙非常厚实牢固，大门旁还有一个雨水箱。我想，对她来说，这里暂时是最安全的地方。于是，我说"伊泽小姐（Izawa）！我想这是安全的地方，有墙，还有水箱。你最好待在这里，等我找辆车来接你。"她点点头。虽然对伊泽小姐（Izawa）这么说似乎很残忍，但我不得不这么说，因为我们处于危机四伏的环境中。

后来我听说，我和她分手后，因为周围都是火，她和碰巧路过的老太太跳进了水箱，心神不安地度过了一夜。第二天，广岛交通局医院的救护车发现并救了她，把她送到医院接受治疗。那天，她的父亲遇难，母亲受伤。如今，她已经痊愈，在广岛一家印刷公司工作，和母亲一起生活。在第一个原子弹轰炸纪念日，她来看我，送给我一包大米表示感谢。那是多么愉快的会面啊！

和伊泽小姐（Izawa）分手后，我开始朝大桥方向跑。路上，我又遇到副主任真岛（Majima）先生，他躺在路上，身旁是他的妻子。她朝我喊，"尾崎（Ozaki）先生！快来救救我丈夫！"幸好，我看到伊达（Date）先生（他后来死了）在路上跑，就喊他来帮助副主任。得到他的同意后，我从附近倒塌的房子那里拿来一块木板，把副主任放在上面，开始抬着他走。走过一个街区，我们找到一幢破碎的房子，那里有宽大花园。我们想这里应该暂时安全，于是进门把他放在花园一角。这时，火已经从两个方向烧起来，我和伊达（Date）先生向副主任和他妻子道别。

真岛（Majima）先生后来怎么样了？两天后，我来到和他分手的地方，没有找到他或他的遗体，也许某个救援团体把他抬去埋在了某个地方。后来，他妻子告诉我，我们分手后五分钟，她丈夫就去世了。唉。她和碰巧路过的行政署长的女儿一起跑向河边，然后来到警察局。她从那里去了东训练场。在东训练场心神不安地度过两个晚上后，她去了住在城市西部的好朋友家。她是日本著名的古典音乐家——"能剧"歌唱家Iwao　Kongo的女儿。

我和副主任夫妻分手，又克服了许多困难后，来到大桥，却过不去了，因为桥那边所有的房屋都在燃烧。我身后也着起了火，于是，我从河岸跳到沙滩上。我手里拿着的帆布背包掉进水里，竟然漂了起来！开始我并没想要把它拿回来。可是，包里的东西是我在这大千世界仅存的一切：银行票据、一些衣物、一些食物还有其它重要的物品。因此，我改变主意，跳进水里，游了约三分钟后，抓住了漂浮的背包。

我坐在沙滩上，考虑自己应该做些什么，可是脑子里一片空白，没有好主意，也没有好计划。在桥下，我发现有约200名难民挤在沙滩上。他们大都受了重伤（特别是脸部），穿着血渍斑斑的破烂衣服，光着脚，没有财物或箱包。后来，一组军人（总共大约5人）扛着军旗过来。其中一名中尉的手受了伤，正在流血。他请我给他包扎，可是我没有布片为他包扎，就撕了一片白衬衫，帮他包上那只流血的手。他向我表示非常感谢。过了一会，这些士兵找到一条小船，举着旗子划船逆流而上。桥那边，火借风势越烧越旺，风将木片吹到河这边，情况非常危险，因此我们常常要跳进水里躲避。这时，我感到饿了，因为那天我没有吃早饭。我发现水面上漂着一个洋葱，就游过去抓住它，然后就着在背包里找到的生米吃掉。我发现，在紧急时刻，吃下任何难吃的东西都能满足胃的需要。

大约早上10点，阴云密布，雨水落到悲惨难民的脸上。这时，我听到连续不断的巨大爆炸声。在场的人们害怕是飞机在轰炸，都在这块狭窄的地方跑来跑去。不久，他们了解到，那是某个弹药库爆炸了。这时，四处都着起大火。我感到非常孤独，以为自己的末日就要到了。但是，我很幸运，河水在渐渐减少，露出了更多的沙滩。我知道，四百多米外就是"东警察局"，就打算到那里寻求即时帮助，于是，开始沿着河岸上的沙滩往前走。

第二章

山丘之上

"一扇门关闭时，便有一扇窗开启。"

—意大利谚语

我走在沙滩上，时不时摔在上面。城里各处都着了火，持续燃烧了一整天，热浪和烟雾笼罩着整个天空和大地。我听到烧毁的房屋倒塌时发出的噼啪声，我看到燃烧的高大树木在空中断裂，闪着电流一样的火花。我看到城市远处的山丘在冒烟，夏日的阳光残忍地照耀在悲惨难民的头上。我看见河滩上的许多难民身体受了伤，情绪低落，在接受熟人和朋友的帮助，用布片包裹着伤口。一位母亲怀抱的婴儿死去。他们的脸上都露出悲惨而无望的表情，预料到麻烦将至。他们该去哪里？失散的姨妈姑妈、兄弟姐妹和挚爱的人们在哪里？接下来的日日夜夜，食物从哪里来？

"我不轻松，不安定，也没休息，可是麻烦还是来了。"

我禁不住抱怨起工作来。

从河滩爬上河岸，我看到四处散落着许多死尸：有男有女，有老有少，有儿童有婴儿，还有狗和猫。有些人半边脸烧焦，有些人被玻璃划伤，他们光着的身子都被烟火熏黑了。我无法忍受眼前这些凄惨的形状。死尸的味道夹杂房屋燃烧散发的烟气，弥漫在空气中和街道上。

我站在河岸高处，环顾四周。火一场接一场地燃烧，房屋一幢接一幢地倒塌，广岛——我们亲爱的城市正在燃烧！我们昂贵的住所即将消失。一切都消失了。广岛不复存在。东边在燃烧，西边在燃烧，四面八方都在燃烧，天气非常炎热。市民死了，被埋葬了；房屋倒塌了；电车和汽车烧着了！从我站的地方往西看，高大的混凝土建筑——中国区报业大厦（Chugoku Press Building）和福屋百货店公司（Fukuya Department Store）的窗户里冲出残忍的火焰。历史悠久的卫理公会派教堂塔（以前我常在星期天去那里）十字架在冒烟。家具和其它室内物品化为灰烬，只有混凝土建筑还保持着自己的形状，自己的结构。我知道，虽然我们广播电台的内部在燃烧，但是它会保留下来，因为它是混凝土建筑。

我终于来到东警察局，可是，没有警官值班，只有几名受伤的警察躺在屋内。我发现一个角落的破损水管中涌出干净的水。高温和夏日的阳光烤得我口干舌燥，我喝了水，感觉它是那么甘甜，一连喝了几杯。办公室附近有几辆要报废的自行车。在这个紧急时刻，我决定不打招呼借一辆自行车，因为根本找不到管事的人。上帝会原谅我的！我确实需要它帮助我逃离火海，躲避危险。于是，我挑了一辆骑上去，多次通过燃烧的街道，越过冒烟的大桥，奔向城市东部。

经历了千难万险，终于来到东训练场。我发现干燥的操场上到处是休息的难民，他们经历了考验，受了伤，几乎裸体，也没有随身的私人物品，一个个筋疲力尽。人们在用木板抬、用肩背着一些受重伤的人。

我躺在草地上，仰望天空，深深地呼吸着新鲜空气。之前，在燃烧的城里一直呼吸着烟雾，因此现在感到这里的空气是那么清新。我感到非常累，考虑着现在该干什么？我记得，曾经有人告诉我，如果广播电台（演播室）在不幸事件中被摧毁，我们应前往位于电台以北约三公里的原村广播电台集合。可是，穿过横河（Yokoyawa）街直达那里的路被火封住了，因此我决定，先从这里绕过原村东部，再翻越小山，度过那条河，抵达目的地，我一定能到达原村的广播电台。

做出决定后，我的心里涌现了一些希望。我躺在广岛东郊，虽然附近房屋远离市区，但是，有些房屋被烧毁，有些房屋的整个屋顶、窗玻璃和某些脆弱部分被炸毁，有些房屋被强大的冲击波震塌了一半……伤员们四处徘徊，大声求救。这里几乎没有未受伤的人，感谢上帝，我安全了。

休息了三十分钟后，我又骑上车，开始上山。那时大约是两点，我感到饿了。我继续往前骑，突然看到路边有幢房子。我不知道里面住的是谁，唐突地走进门去。屋里有位中年妇女和一个小姑娘。每个房间里都有许多难民。我向他们说明自己如何逃离燃烧的城市，并表示希望能休息一会。他们把我让进一个房间，好心地给我送上蛋糕和茶。因为我的帆布背包里还有一些大米，就用那位妇女给我的土豆自己烧了饭。吃完饭，我向他们道别，又骑车上了山。路上，我看到许多海军卡车拉着很多受伤的人，沿着山路朝北急驶。难民们近乎裸体，他们的脸部和头发被烧焦，有些人穿着血渍斑斑的衣服，使我无法认清他们是男是女。

一辆汽车慢慢地跟在我后面，我朝车里看了一眼，看到一位贵族军官躺在里面。他的脸部受伤，包了起来。我后来听说，他是在陆军服役的朝鲜王子。原子弹落下那天，他在相生桥（Aioi Bridge）附近骑马，受了重伤。他的副官认为自己不在主人身边，负有责任，就自杀了。路上有一所小学，许多难民聚集在那里。伤员们在那里接受治疗并得到施舍的饼干或米饭。

这时，山路越来越陡，我下了自行车，开始步行。一辆满载伤员的卡车疾驶而来。突然，卡车上有位妇女喊出我的名字，

"尾崎（Ozaki）先生！尾崎（Ozaki）先生！"

"你是谁？"我感到奇怪。

"我是山崎（Yamazaki），广播电台的职员。我的背部受了重伤。"她说。

她坐在卡车中央，只披了两片布，面露悲伤。

"噢，是你！照顾好自己。上帝会帮助你的！我一定会跟主任说你的事。请稍等一等。"

卡车开过去，不见了。接受治疗后，她恢复了健康，现在还在我们广播电台工作。

路上，又我遇到我们广播电台的两名女职员，其中一人因为脚受了伤，拄着棍子。我问她们是怎么从电台走过来的。她们告诉我，她们到河边时，正好附近有条船，就坐船过了河，翻过Ushida山，走上这条路。我为她们感到庆幸，然后与她们分手，因为她们要到附近村庄的朋友家去。

大约一个小时后，我来到河边。我必须过河。河边有条渡船，划船的男孩和善地把我和我的自行车接到船上。登上河对岸时，我问他需要多少钱。

"钱？你认为我能找难民要钱吗？我猜你是从广岛来的，我能找难民要钱吗？我必须帮助你。"

我非常感动，感觉眼睛湿润了。他知道，他的同胞正在遭受这场灾难的折磨！

　　我上了岸，已经是黄昏。我问村民去原村广播电台怎么走，他们告诉我骑车要二十分钟。这时，一辆卡车向广岛方向疾驶，车上装着食物和给养。经过我身旁时，车上有人朝我扔了什么东西。我发现那是一些饼干，就向他们表示感谢，把它当作是来自天堂的礼物。傍晚6点30分，我安全到达原村广播电台。从广岛来的同事大约已有十人到了那里，正等着其余工作人员的到来。他们都对这件大事感到困惑不解。主任来了，我向他详细说明了自己的所有经历。原村电台的朋友们向我表示欢迎，给了我一条毛巾和其它物品，并给我上了一盘热米饭和汤。

　　我发现，虽然这个电台离广岛约有五公里，但是也遭到了原子弹的破坏。冲击波震碎了窗玻璃和办公室的屋顶，让我知道了原子弹的威力有多大。电台办公室周围有个宽大的花园。我来到花园。黑暗中，我看到胡枝子已经在花园各处绽放花朵。这里很安静，但是，在约五公里远的南方天空，我看到熊熊大火仍然焚烧着那座城市，映得天空像白天一样明亮。

　　那是广岛！我亲爱的城市，我们的家园！我跪在草地上，向上帝祈求平安，为家中的母亲、为在城市附近一家工厂上班的、我唯一的儿子精一（Sei-ichi），为我的朋友及其当时尚未找到的家人祈求平安。这是广岛的末日吗？这是我生命的终结吗？我祈祷，我感觉到上帝的帮助。虽然遭遇了灾难和不幸，上帝依然在我身边。我们还有一些房间可以入住，日本这个地区的某个角落还有一些避难所可以入住。灾难使我坚强起来。我想起《圣经》里的一些诗句——

　　"但是，我们也以经历苦难为荣；我们知道经历苦难修得耐性，由耐性而得经验，由经验而得希望——"

　　是的！有经验就有希望！寒风把我从沉思中唤醒。我回到屋里，准备裹着毛毯在硬地板上睡觉。可是，我无法入睡，心神不宁地过了那一夜。

第三章

寻找亲人

"显然，环境本身不会使我们快乐或不快乐。我们的感觉取决于我们对环境作出反应的方式。我们都能承受灾难，战胜灾难——如果必须这么做的话——我们比我们想像的更强大。"

— 戴尔·卡耐基

我睡眼朦胧地起了床，感觉浑身懒洋洋的。在正常情况下，人们能够以正确的方式处理问题，但是，在紧急情况下，你很难按照需要去选择正确的方法。面对灾难却不知所措，就无法应对灾难。在寒冷的晨风吹拂下，我们清醒过来，想到了必须做的第一件事。这天早上我们必须做的，就是让我们在东京的广播电台了解我们遭遇的紧急事件。然而，大多数长途电话线路和其它发送线路都被冲击波切断了，不过，我们发现还可以借助姬路市中转，连接广岛与东京之间的线路。于是，我们发出一则短消息，"城市遭飞机攻击摧毁；我们的广播电台着了火；许多工作人员死亡；遭受重大的致命损伤，等等。"我们的广播电台有许多事要处理。可是，如前所述，所有的发送线路和长途电话线路都被摧毁了，因此，我们决定，接下来，一边等待来自邻近电台和东京的帮助，一边寻找失散的工作人员和家人。

为了寻找家人，我离开电台，骑上自行车返回广岛。通往广岛的公路上挤满了人，我难以骑车前行。这些人有的来自广岛，有的前往广岛；有的人受了伤，有的人背着沉重的帆布背包；汽车、四轮马车和卡车上挤满难民和物品；有些人因受到此次突发事件的刺激而异常兴奋，有些人因疲劳和夏季的炎热而无精打采。我来到城市的入口横河。那里停着一辆装满食物和给养的卡车；有人叫住我，给了我捐赠的大米。从这里开始，更难骑车前行，因为有许多倒地的电线杆、倒塌的房屋和大量木材碎石挡住了去路，一座座大桥坍塌、被焚毁。我无法沿着往常的道路直接回家，不得不多次改变路线，绕道而行，有时还要跨越冒着浓烟的大桥；我常常被绊倒，但是无论如何我要到西桥（West-bridge）——我家就在那附近。我看到街道上、河水里有无数具尸首。在西电话局附近的路上，我听见一个防空洞里传来非常微弱的声音。我朝里面看去，发现有几个受了重伤的裸体女孩相拥在一起，她们的皮肤都被烧焦了；她们大都好像就要死了。我听到一个女孩用非常虚弱的声音呼喊着"妈妈！妈妈！"我问她的名字，可是，没有回音。我无法帮助她们，因为我没有办法救她们。因此，我闭上眼睛，为她们祈祷。附近有位妇女，怀里抱着一个婴儿，边哭边走。我知道，那个婴儿已经死了。

我终于到大桥附近的家了，却发现它已经化为灰烬。这是我一生中最痛苦的经历。我开始推开灰烬、碎石及其它金属，很怕在下面某个地方会找到母亲的遗体。突然，我听到身后响起一个声音——

"奶奶是安全的。"

听到这句话，我大吃一惊。那是我儿子，他安全而健康。我们泪流满面地拥抱在一起。感谢上帝。他解释说：在工厂听到爆炸声时，他被冲击波撞倒，但是没有受伤。他急忙跑回家，这里离工厂只有20分钟路程；到家时，我们的房子在燃烧，奶奶和邻居站在门口。他找到一辆马车，让奶奶和邻居坐上，就朝桥对面最近的村子逃。走了约二十分钟，巧遇一辆储备卡车，把他们送到城外约十公里的Jigogen渔村。现在，他们呆在一所小学里。

听了儿子的报告，我非常开心，立刻决定去那里看望我母亲。我们徒步走到Jigogen村时已近傍晚。校舍里挤满了难民。我在操场一角找到母亲。她左脚受了伤，正在一块垫子上休息，不知为什么很兴奋。看到我安然无恙，她非常高兴。

有人给了我们米饭和汤，还捐给我们衣服和衬衫。因为学校房间内很拥挤，还有些人濒临死亡，我们决定在操场过夜。但是，因为受到此次突发事件的刺激和蚊虫的叮咬，我们根本无法入睡。

第四章

焚毁的城市

"人在磨难中成长。"

—— 布莱斯·帕斯卡

8月8日清晨，阳光普照。我把母亲和儿子交给负责的官员照顾，向他们道了别，因为我在广播电台还有许多事情要做。

我来到市中心。天哪！一片荒漠！人们现在称那里为"原子荒漠"：没有居民，没有树木，没有任何生物；所有的电车都停了，随处可见被烧毁的电车。死亡的气息弥漫在街头和空气里。在原子弹爆炸中心附近，坚固钢筋混凝土结构的相生桥（Aioi Bridge）被炸成几段，厚实的铁金属被折弯，桥体被摧毁。我听说，在那一刹那，广岛邮政局约有200名工作人员被埋葬，死了，只有两三人获救。大约600名县政府官员也遭遇了同样的命运。那天，一辆电车正巧驶近爆炸中心，所有乘客都在一瞬间死去！这实在是人类历史上付出的最大牺牲。

我来到福屋百货公司（Fukuya Department Store），那里原有的绚丽灯光和女店员欢快的声音都不复存在。滚滚的浓烟和炽热的火焰掠过之后，只留下水泥外墙和地板。我来到十字路口，那里是劝业银行（Kangyo Bank）所在地，有许多受重伤的市民躺在银行的地上。他们中大多数人烧伤了面部皮肤，所有人都在尖叫和哭泣。有一些医生和护士在帮他们包扎伤口，给他们打针。

最后，我来到我们的广播电台。后面那间新建的木质办公室不见了，但主建筑还在。我从前门走进去，看到所有的广播机器和橱柜都被炸碎，家具、书籍、唱片均化为灰烬。水从破裂的水管中涌出，淌了一地。我走进节目部的房间，这里除了金属，一切都变成了灰烬，房间似乎比以前更宽敞。我找到一个以前用过的军用饭盒，拿走留作纪念。接着，我走进防空洞，找出所有重要的物品，有私人的，也有公家的。它们不是被烧焦，就是浸满了水。我爬上电台屋顶，环顾四周。那里是一片荒漠，什么也没留下，只有一些混凝土建筑或烧了一半的树木。看上去远处的比治山（Hijiyama）山近在眼前。

在前往原村广播电台的路上，我去看了原来的军事基地所在地老城堡。那里不再有城堡，也没有了军队营房。我发现训练场和老城堡周围的池塘里躺着许多士兵的尸体。城堡的遗迹和石块还有烧了一半的树木只显示了士兵们曾经辉煌的梦想。军国主义和封建主义都消失了。我在烧焦的草地上徘徊了一会，回忆着过去的岁月。

傍晚，我回到原村广播电台。我们决定在电台附近为我们的工作人员借几间民房。虽然我们电台有约三十五名工作人员死去，但是幸运的是节目部所有的干事都安全。只有几个人受了轻伤，失去了妻子或孩子。

如前所述，关于落在广岛的大炸弹，有许多种传言。日本总司令部只简单地宣称，有一颗威力巨大的科学炸弹落在广岛市，导致人员和房屋的重大损伤。后来，我们通过来自美国的情报得知，是原子弹导致了这场大灾难，我们也才明白，大多数人员的伤亡是由辐射引起的。

谣言四起，宣称七十五年内，广岛及其郊区不可能有生物、人类或树木生存。因此，仍留在破碎的房屋和城里防空洞中的难民动身前往国内其它地方。说实话，死亡人数在增加。遭到辐射的市民发现自己的头发开始脱落，皮肤上出现了斑点，他们一天天死去。有些人死于血液受到辐射造成的感染。由于所有的火葬场都被摧毁，城里的死者家属不得不亲手埋葬死去的亲人。

广岛事件发生后，几天之内，世界上又发生了两起最大事件——第二颗原子弹降落长崎；俄国军队进攻并涌入满州里，俄国正式向日本宣战。灾难接着灾难。我们如何承受得起如此沉重的打击？日本的末日就要到了。陆军和海军失去了激励日本和日本人民的力量。

大约在这时，我们被告知，日本在与盟军进行和平谈判。后来，我们接到通知，8月15日正午，天皇陛下将宣布重大通知，要求所有车辆都在那个时刻停下来，收听这个通知。我们忙着把公告发出去。我国人民都焦急地等待着那一时刻的到来。

那一天，所有的车辆和街上的行人都停了下来，在家里和在办公室的人们急不可待地收听广播。东京的播音员首先做了介绍，接着，我们听到天皇的声音。我们知道，战争就要结束了！而那是无条件投降！我无法用笔描述那个历史时刻给人们留下的深刻印象，也无法说清我们是什么感受，更不知道以后这块土地上会发生什么。所有的人都哭了，百感交集地哭了。所有的服役人员都获得释放，开始从国外返回。战争期间从城市搬到农村的人们准备返回家园，返回烧焦的城市；所有的火车、轮船和汽车上都挤满了返乡的人，所有人都背着大帆布背包。在盟军登陆这片海滨之前，有一段时间，车上、街上一片混乱。

说点我自己的事：我母亲又回到广岛，住在一幢毁了一半的房子里。她的脚受了重伤，于9月1日清晨去世。我和儿子在她的尸体上浇上燃料，点着了火！这么做似乎很残忍，但是在那个紧急时刻，我不得不这么做。上帝知道。为了埋葬她的遗骸，我准备去濑户内海那边的四国老家。9月17日午夜，一场大洪水不期而至。大雨持续下了几天，午夜，我被哭喊声惊醒，"洪水！洪水！"我打开窗户。啊！水就要涨到我们所在的村舍二楼了。要是洪流冲走了房屋会怎么样？我看到汹涌的洪水上漂着许多圆木和破碎的房屋。我们没有办法逃生，只能等着洪水退去，等着黎明到来。我们很幸运，随着黎明的到来，水位开始渐渐降低。

黎明时分，水位降至约60厘米，我们感到自己安全了。火灾接着洪灾！据说，由于洪水的破坏，农作物和蔬菜的收成将会减少。我们的心沉了下来。

因为带着母亲的遗骸，那天下午，我和儿子在洪水中冒险前往约六公里以南的海港。我们经历了许多困难，多次趟过洪流，到城里时，已经是深夜。那里没有居民，是一座黑暗的死城。我们找到一辆破败的电车，在里面休息了约两小时，又开始朝海港走。第二天一早，我们搭乘一艘小船前往老家，埋葬母亲的遗骸。

那年秋天一个明媚的日子，占领军士兵抵达吴市——以前的军港。新时代到来了！

第五章

和平降临

"吾人无意奴役日本民族或消灭其国家……日本政府必须将阻止日本人民民主趋势之复兴及增强之所有障碍予以消除。"

— 摘自《波茨坦宣言》

从那难忘的日子——第一颗原子弹落到广岛的土地上——以后，四年过去了。如今，日本不再有战争，而且作为民主国家迈开了第一步。一切都变了！日本的封建制度灭亡了！1947年11月3日，日本宣布了新宪法，确定了"言论、宗教和思想自由，尊重基本的人权"。服役的人们获得释放。所有海外士兵，从中国、西伯利亚和南太平洋回到他们被烧焦、被破坏的家乡。陆军和海军完全解除了武装，日本失去了许多殖民地，其主权也只限于原有的群岛。因此，在不久的将来，日本的战后人口将在这片小小的土地上发展到八千万。但是，那里的政治和社会状况混乱了一段时间。因为通货膨胀，日常生活一天比一天艰难，黑市到处泛滥。由于房屋、食品和衣物稀少，物价一天天升高。小偷，抢劫犯和杀人犯塞满了警察局的牢房。不稳定的日子，不眠之夜持续的时间越来越长。尤其是那些接受了军事教育和训练的年轻人，似乎失去了生活的目标。他们还误解了民主的真正含意，生活方式变得粗糙无序。他们在街道或黑市间游荡，或者成群结队地入室抢劫。

书摊上卖着廉价淫荡的书籍、杂志和印刷品。家庭主妇不得不去农场，从农民手中购买大米、谷物和蔬菜，用他们必需的衣物换取食物。

日本确实面临着无秩序的严酷考验。不过，从第三年下半年开始，社会状况已经略有好转。盟军——尤其是美军和英军——向我们伸出了援助之手，他们向这片海滨运送了食物、衣物和其它物品；联合国善后经济总署（UNRRA）和亚洲救援公认机构（LARA）提供的货物也为孤儿、寡妇和无家可归的人们带来了生机；食物越来越多，衣物得到补充，房屋也建好了。

希望和重建！虽然经历了重重灾难，我们必须实现为他们制定的新计划。现在，广岛拥有245,000名居民（原子弹轰炸前为312,200人），60,000幢房屋（那天之前为76,000幢）；百货公司、银行、电影秀场以及官方和私营出版社已经开始工作；电车开始运营；温暖的茶室和雅致的咖啡馆、餐馆已经开门迎客。

来自海外的船只载满货物进了宇吉（Ujina）港。每天都有外国人前来参观"原子城"废墟，想知道原子弹的威力到底有多大。广岛正在复苏。如今，"广岛悲剧不再重演"的运动活跃在世界，也活跃在日本。

如今，我们满怀喜悦和希望响应日本新宪法向热爱和平人们发出的声明，"日本人民永远放弃利用国家主权权力发动战争，永远不以武力威胁或行使武力作为解决国际争端的手段"因此，这不是广岛的末日，这是它的第一个充满希望的日子。

— 结束 —

THE SONG OF
HIROSHIMA

ORIGINAL DOCUMENT

Program Section,
Hiroshima Central Broadcasting
Station, Hiroshima
March 27, '49

Dear Mr. Crews, —

Pardon me my rudeness that I am going to write to you for the first time. I am a secretary in charge of communications and translation in our station. I know you came to this city at the middle of last month, and giving us good suggestions and direction about broadcasting job. Now if you mind, will you read my poorly done notes about the recollection of the first atom-bomb fell at Hiroshima which I have recently written and here I have enclosed. I have heard you are returning to the States next April. I am very glad, if you would use this material, when you speak and write about Japan over there. Anyhow I am glad if you have time to read my poor notes and take it to your country.

P.S. Mr. Kodama of our station
Kindly take this letter and
the notes to you.

Yours Sincerely
A. Ozaki

NOTE BOOK

The Song of Hiroshima
— the sixth of August, 1945 —

By Atsuhiro Ozaki
Program Section, Hiroshima
Central Broadcasting Station,
Hiroshima, Japan.

⟨金野便都市 の定額⟩

The song of Hiroshima
— the Sixth of August 1945 —

By Atsuhiro Ozaki
Program Section, Hiroshima
Central Broadcasting Station,
Hiroshima, Japan.

Contents :

Forwards
Chapter I   The Day.
Chapter II   Over the Hill.
Chapter III   Seeking after the Beloved ones.
Chapter IV   The Burnt City.
Chapter V   The Peace Has Come.

Forward

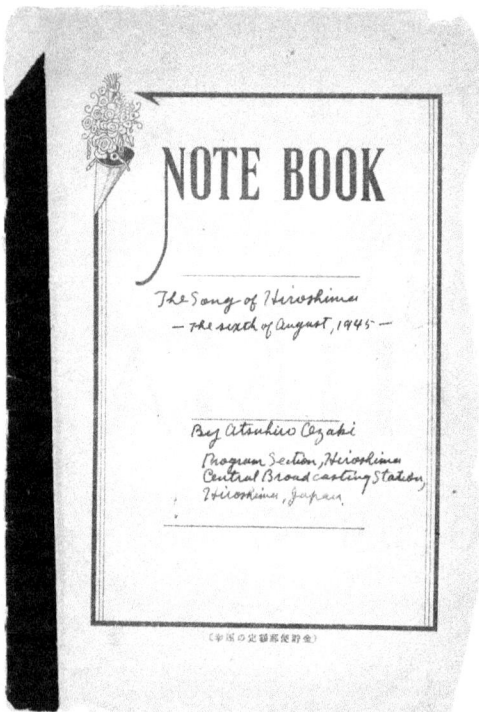

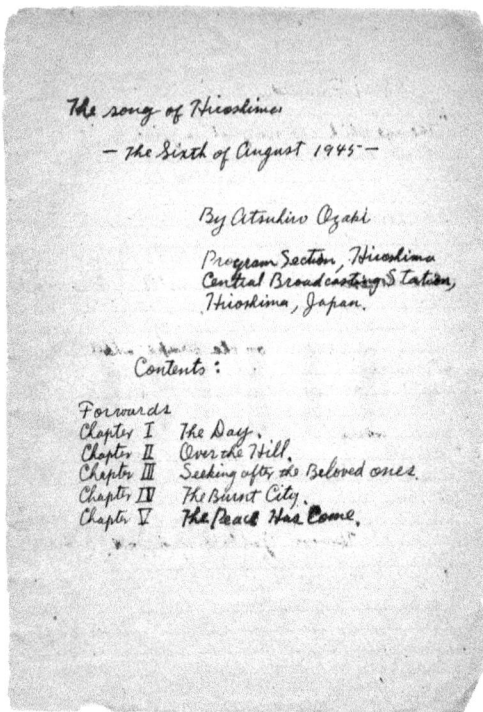

"The age which has no great anguish on its
heart, has no great music in its life"
— Karl Barth —

The fourth memorial of the unforgettable day,
when the first Atom-bomb, in the pages of history,
fell on the soil and streets of our dear Hiroshima,
where the seven rivers with crystal water are
still flowing, on August 6, 1945, is coming in a
few months. Now it is Spring; the cherry-blossoms
as before are blooming on the banks, where our
beloved ones used to stroll; the larks are still
singing in the sky; and from the frozen soil the
greens are peeping out again. Flowers on the
graves where our beloved ones lay, opened
many times and faded away. Nature is unchangeable, but human beings have changed;
our once beloved ones are no more and our
old homes with cosy rooms and dear furniture
are gone! However, God takes and gives. Some
of us remain in spite of the trial, leaving
hope and strength to live on;
The new day started at that historical
moment, from the destruction and the ashes left
by the Atom-bomb, the survivals got up for the
new day, full of "freedom from fear." From the

---

windows of the newly-built, narrow barrack,
bright lights are shining on the burned gardens,
and the melodies of "the Song of the Reconstruction
of Hiroshima" are echoing in the dark starry sky,

"Let's reconstruct Hiroshima,
It's daybreak and morning, we are cheerful;
Sounds of hammers are echoing
         in the morning wind,
Hope arising from the Atom Desert."

Yes! reconstruction and hope.

Now, let me explain why I am going to
write this note; on the morning of the unforgettable day, I was working at the office
of the Hiroshima Central Broadcasting Station,
which was located within one kilometre of
the center where the first Atom-bomb fell.
About thirty-five of my co-workers were killed,
and my dear mother who was in our home
in the suburbs of the city passed away
after a serious injury, too. Luckily for me
I was safe, not slightly injured, because
I was in a room enclosed by a thick
wall. What a bitter experience it was to
lose my dear mother, my home, my
furniture, my favorite books and

belongings and also the office where I had worked. Is there such a great event recorded in human history, which resulted in so much loss in one moment?

At that time Hiroshima had about 366,000 inhabitants. By the first Atom-bomb 92,133 citizens died by radiation or by being crushed under houses; 9,428 people were seriously wounded, 27,997 were slightly injured; survivals numbered 176,987, and 8,200 houses (90% of the city) were burnt to ashes; the percentage of the dead by radiation increased daily to 70,000 from 46,185. (In these figures the soldiers and service men are not included) And well-known sites and precious historical monuments and building are gone! All gone! and our beloved ones and all things faded away at one moment!

Storm comes after storm; beside this disaster, within about one month, on September 17th, a great flood came to this part of Japan like a ghost and great damage was done. (1,199 persons died or drowned, 897 unknown, and other great damage of houses and rural lands)

Sometimes in the post-war period, I have talked with my friends in our office, that we should record such a terrible experience and event

as materials for the coming generation, though we were poor in writing or could not mention what we intended to do. However, at that time we were very busy setting up new houses, reconstructing our lives and our job at the broadcasting station, and almost four years have passed like a dream. But it is not a dream; it is a fact that there will be no more strife or wars among mankind in the future.

Peace has come to this feudal country where our comrades suffered long under oppressor and dictator! A new age has indeed come! As for me, what I saw with my eyes and heard with my ears and what I experienced with my whole being on that day, I must write in memo, or diary; it's my duty to our country and to the peace-loving people of the world,

> "I for Japan,
> Japan for the world,
> The world for Christ,
> And all for God
> —Kanzo Uchimura

Indeed this is a human document, intending to mention the vivid events and the true facts which took place on the morning of the First Atom-bomb falling on the city. However I am afraid, by my poor knowledge of English, I can't sketch rightly what I experienced, but the narration of the fact itself would prove what happened truly. About scientifical, medical research, someone else must do; my aim is to describe only my personal record of it.

As to my professional career, after being graduated from Kwansei Gakuin, a Methodist Church University, founded by Dr. Lambuth an American missionary, I was once a pastor, an English teacher, a newspaperman, and am now a radio man of the Hiroshima Central Broadcasting Station, living in a humble cottage on the Atom Desert, being an usual civilian, enjoying the daily life of New Japan.

Chapter I. The Day

"Christian joy is enhanced by suffering.
—Peak—

It was indeed the sixth of August, 1945. Hot and bright days had continued, but by the attacks of the U.S. Planes day by day, and night after night, most important points and cities were crushed or burned to ashes; in the latter part of 1944 already Tokyo and its suburbs had received several attacks and terrible damage. America had taken Marikkuna Isles; and from there B29s freely attacked our cities and important points. January 3, 1945, 90 planes came to Nagoya; Taiwan and Okinawa were attacked; and bombed by 500 carrier-planes; January 30, U.S. Army and Navy ventured to land at Manila Bay; on the 16th of February U.S. Task Forces landed on Iwojima Island where the most terrible fights in history were held. On March 13th Osaka and 17th Kobe received much damage and fire respectively, and on the 21st of the same month, Iwo-shima was captured at last last by U.S. Task Forces after the loss of many lives and guns on both sides. By this time most of the important cities and bases of these islands will attacked by B 29s. or **carier-planes**; and houses and important points burned and destroyed; people loitered about without their clothes, or food. Where could she lost sheep go? Japan was in the agony of her last day — death.

With these reports and news we were in a melancholy mood and gradually were becoming aware of the coming miserable fortune and dark **days**. The leaders of the Government tried to make the people believe in the final victory; but they cried out in vain.

Now the day was very hot from the morning. At that time the work **which I was in charge** of the radio station was that of air-defence communications, receiving the news of the where-abouts of the enemy's planes, from both Military and Naval bases of Hiroshima and Kure, and after writing up hurriedly and roughly the content I received, I used to hurry the scripts to the announcer who **was** impatiently waiting by my side; to put them on the air. These jobs lasted about two years from morning till night, having no time to rest, and always nervously

answering the bells of the telephones.

At two o'clock in that morning on an air-raid warning was announced, two enemies' new planes were flying over Hiroshima Districts, but about 6 o'clock it was released, though the enemy's planes were still near Hiroshima. There was a misunderstanding of the officer in charge of the case; **by the release**, the citizens who had run away out of the city the previous night and who had been in the air-raid shelters came home; and were taking breakfast or preparing to go to offices or factories; and some were already on the streets or in the gardens, being refreshed by the morning breezes after fears and fatigues from the previous night. As it is the natural Japanese custom, in the hot Summer season especially men and boys who are staying in doors are naked putting on no clothes or simply putting on Japanese yukata (some simple Summer clothes) or short-pants.

At that very moment, when the clock pointed to nearly 8.15 A.M. the first Atom-bomb in the history fell on the land of Hiroshima! The centre of it was somewhere near the Aioi-bridge, almost at the centre of the city. Luckily for me, as the telephone from the Military base rang loudly, (it was

about 8 A.M) I dashed into the air-defence communications room with two announcers to receive information, and when I had finished filling up the news-blank and handed it to the announcer in charge, I heard a great sound, with the screeming of men for help, and at the same time some crumbs of ceiling fell upon my head; and I saw also some current of blue light something like accetylne light which entered and covered the whole room. I felt that our station had received a direct hit.

Covering my head with a cushion which was on the chair, and trembling with fear of what the world would become, I rushed into the room of the Program Section; lo! the room had changed! There was no room to step in, because most of the desks and chairs and other pieces of furniture as well as window-glass were broken and fallen; some of my co-workers had fallen on the floor with their faces and bodies injured very much by the bomb-blast. Blood was gushing from their faces and hands; someone was screaming for help, as his eye was cut by a piece of glass caused by the blast. In their calamity I did not know what to do. A certain

newspaper man of the Dōmei Tsushinsha

(a well-known Japanese news agency before the War) dashed to me naked and asked me for something to put on. So I gave him a khaki uniform which happened to be there. As for me I hurried up to my desk and luckily for me I found my cap, my suit, and a rucksack which contained my personal belongings for an urgent occasion.

After a moment, all the workers over there were picking up their clothes and personal things and preparing to run away, in spite of their wounds on head or hands or feet; some already had run away to some safer places. A fire broke out from some corner of the station, but it was put out by the pumps.

I looked out from the broken window, lo! all the wooden houses in my sight had fallen down or were crushed into pieces and from somewhere smoke and fire already were arising. I wondered what had happened. On the street before the radio station I saw many citizens who were wounded seriously, almost with naked bodies or only shirts or short pants running to the north of the city in groups or alone.

intimates or friends were helping or carrying by hand the seriously wounded men and women, and children in agony of pain, and from their faces or hands or breasts, I saw blood gushing. Children were calling out the names of their lost parents and brothers in vain. Some were running on the street with not a piece of clothing on their injured bodies. When I saw how the citizens were suffering from the disaster, I recollected some terrible passages and scenes of Dante's Inferno in "Paradise Lost" that I read when I was young.

I recognized that all the city was destroyed, but could not understand why we had such a terrible and miserable result in one moment; it was a mystery; and no one knew the truth at that urgent moment, only coming to the vague conclusion that a powerful, large bomb had fallen on the ground or some special electrical power had prevailed upon the city and the suburbs by some scientific means.

In this calamity, however, I came to myself, and contrived some way to get from this dangerous place to an other safer shelter. I first thought of my sick mother and

of my only son in the factory, but fire had already broken out in that part of the city and I could not return there. God may protect them! So through the Sakae-bridge, which is nearest to our station, I intended to go to "the Eastern Drill Ground." As soon my decision was settled, I hurriedly prepared to put on my suit and the rucksack. And on my way down to the first floor I discovered a girl announcer, Miss Izawa lying on the floor, who could not walk after receiving a bruise on the foot. With my friends I carried her to the gate, where I found Mr. Majima, Sub-chief of the Program Section lying with bloody body, calling for help; some were there surrounding him.

At that time a certain girl held my hand and requested me to save her father who was crushed under the timbers and could not move, while several friends were calling out to be saved. And a child about two years old was crying out, seeking her lost mother near the gate. I was at a loss what I should do. But I made up my minds to help first the girl announcer and our chief; so with the help of my friends I put a board on a baby-carriage which

fortunately I found near the gate, and upon it we let them lay. But they were too heavy and it crushed immediately, causing the two wounded ones to fall on the ground. So as to the chief, I put him under the care of my friends while I determined to carry the girl on my shoulder. But she was so heavy and the heat of the summer sun was so severe that it was very difficult to carry her on my shoulder; besides these, the road was full of fallen timbers and poles and spreading breakstones.

Carrying the girl, I walked about two blocks after stumbling and falling on the ground two or three times because she was so heavy. At this times few people were running away and from several places near-by a fire arose. We stopped before the gate of a great mansion owned by Mr. Awaya, the chief Administrator of the Chugoku Districts. I discovered the walls of it were very thick and strong; and also beside the gate there was a rain-water tank. I reckoned that this would be the safest place for her for a while, saying

"Miss Izawa! I guess this is a safe place; there are wall and a water-tank. You better wait until I shall find a

vehicle to carry you" she nodded. Though it seemed to be cruel to say this to Miss Izawa, I could not help saying so, because danger was surrounding us.

After I parted with her, I was told afterwards, as she was surrounded with fire, she jumped into the water-tank with an old woman who happened to pass by and they spent the night in the tank un-easily and next day she was found and was saved by the rescue car of the Hiroshima Communication Bureau's Hospital and was carried to the hospital and was healed, while her father died on that day and also her mother was wounded. But now she was has recovered and is working as a clerk in a certain Printing Co., in Hiroshima and living with her mother. On the first Memorial Day of the Atom-bomb falling, she called on me and thanked me with a bundle of rice. What a happy meeting it was!

After I parted with the girl, I began to run in the direction of the Bridge. On my way there I found again Mr. Majima our chief, lying on the road and by him I found his wife there, crying out to me,

"Mr. Ozaki! Come and help my husband!" Luckily, I saw Mr. Date (who afterwards died)

running along the road. I called and requested him to help our chief; as he consented I brought a board from a near-by broken house and put our chief on it, and we began to carry him. After we walked about one block, we found a burned house with a broad garden. We thought this would be a safe shelter for a moment, so we entered the gate and put him down in one corner of the garden. By this time fire had come from two directions; so with Mr. Date, we said good-by to our chief and his wife.

What happened to Mr. Majima afterwards; When I went to the spot where we parted with him after two days, I did not find him or his remains; may be some rescue party had carried him to bury him in some place. As to his wife, she afterwards explained to me that after we parted with them her husband passed away within five minutes; so she ran with the daughter of the chief-administitution who happened to to pass by, to the river and then to the police station and there she went to the East Drill Ground, and after passing uneasily two nights over there she went to her intimate friend's home out of the city. She is a daughter of Mr. Kongo, Jūrō, a well-known Japanese classic music, "Noh Song" singer.

After I parted with my chief and his wife, with much difficulty, I came to the Bridge, but I could not cross it, because all the houses beyond the bridge were burning. And from behind me fire broke out too, so I jumped down upon the sands from the bank of the River. My rucksack which I was holding in my hand fell into the water; it floated! At first I thought I would give up trying to get it. But the contents of it was everything I had in this wide, wide world; bank notes, some clothes, some food, and other important belongings it contained; therefore I changed my mind and jumped into the water, caught the floating bag after swimming about three minutes.

I sat down on the sands and thought what I should do and no good ideas or plans came into my mind. Under the bridge I found about 200 refugees clustered on the sands. Most of them were wearing torn bloody clothes and were seriously injured, especially their faces, and also they were barefooted and had no clothes belongings or rags. Then a group of military men (about five in all) came holding a regimental flag. A certain lieutenant among them had his hand wounded and

it was bleeding; he asked me to bind his hand; as I had not a piece of cloth to bind it, I tore a piece of my white shirt and bound the bloody hand. He thanked me very much. After a while, these soldiers found a little boat and holding the flag they rowed up the river. The fire beyond the bridge was fanned by a strong wind and pieces of timber blew to this part of the river; as it was very dangerous, we jumped frequently into the water to get out of it. By this time I felt very hungry, because I had not taken breakfast that morning. I found a piece of onion floating on the water, I caught it after swimming. And ate it with some raw rice which I had found in my rucksack. I discovered, in an urgent time any poor thing to eat could satisfy the stomach.

About 10 o'clock in the morning, rains with dark clouds began to fall upon the faces of the miserable refugees. At this time I heard some great sounds of bombing continually. People on that spot feared they might be some attacks from planes; and they ran about on the narrow place here and there but soon they were informed that they were the explosions of

a certain powder magazine. By this time fire was in every direction. I felt very lonely, thinking my end was coming, But luckily going out of ... the river was gradually going down and more and more sands appeared. Over there a quarter of a mile away, I knew that there was "The East Police Station" and I had intended to go to the station to receive instant help; so I began to walk down on the sands along the bank.

Chapter II

Over the Hill

When a gate closes, a window opens.
— an Italian proverb

I walked on the sands; sometimes jumped on them. Fire in every part of the city lasted the rest of the day; glaring heat and smoke covered the whole sky and land. I heard the sounds of cracking of the falling houses caused by fire; tall trees were burning and breaking up in the sky, sparking like electric currents. I saw the hill beyond the city smoking. The Summer sun cruelly shone upon the heads of the miserable people. I saw on the sands of the river many refugees, wounded and depressed in spirit, intimates and friends helping them, binding the wounded with some pieces of cloth; a baby in the hands of its mother passing away; their countenances expecting coming troubles were covered with miserable and hopeless moods. Where would they go? Where could the lost parents, brothers and sisters and be-loved ones be now? How would food for the coming day and night be supplied?

"I am not at ease, neither am I quiet, neither have I rest; but trouble cometh."

With Job I could not help complaining.

I climbed upon the bank from the sands of the River. Here and there I saw a great many dead; men and women, old and young, children and babies as well as dogs and cats; some with half of their faces burned; some cut by pieces of glass and being naked, and blackened by smoke and fire. I could not bear

to see these miserable shapes. The smell of the dead mixed with the smoke of burning houses prevailed in the air and on the streets.

I stood on the high place of the bank and looked around. Fire after fire, crush after crush. Hiroshima, our dear city is burning! Our dear abode is coming to the very end. All gone. No more! Hiroshima! Fire in the east and fire in the west. And from every direction. It's very hot. The citizens had died and were buried; houses falling, tram-cars and motor-cars burning. West of where I stood, I saw a cruel glare of fire current pushing out from the windows of the tall concrete Chugoku Press Building and the giant Fukuya Department Store. The cross of the longer Tower of the Methodist Church where I used to go on Sundays was smoking. Only the concrete buildings kept their shape or structure, though the furniture and other things in doors were burned ashes. I knew our radio station would remain in spite of the burning of the inner part, as it was a concrete one.

At last I came to the East Station, but there were no officers on duty; several wounded policemen were lying in the room. In a corner I found fresh water gushing out from a broken supply. I drank. It was so sweet after thirst by heat and the summer sun, that I drank several cups of it. Near the office there were several bicycles which were going to burn. I made up my mind to borrow a bicycle without permission at this urgent time, because there were none to ask about it. God would pardon me! I did need it to get away from the fire and the danger. So picking up one I rode on to the eastern part of the city, through the burning streets and crossing smoking bridges many times. After many difficulties, at last I came to the Eastern Drill Ground, where I found here and there a group of refugees resting on the dry ground, all fatigued after the trial, being wounded, and almost naked and having no personal belongings with them. People were carrying some seriously wounded persons on boards or on their shoulders.

I lay down on the grass, and looking up into the sky, I breathed deeply the fresh air. It was so fresh as I had been breathing the smoky air in the burning city. I felt I was very tired and was thinking what to do now? I remembered I had been told that if our broadcasting station (the studio) was destroyed on a tragic occasion we would remove and gather at the Hara Broadcasting Station, which was located about two miles northward from our studio. But the quiet way there through Yokogawa Street had been closed by fire; so I decided to reach the destination at first by going around the east side of the Hara Village from here and then passing over the hill and crossing the River, I would reach the station in Hara.

As I decided to do so, I felt some hope arising in my heart. This place where I lay down was in the eastern suburbs of Hiroshima. Though the houses near-by were far away from the city, some burned or all the roofs, window-glass and some weak parts of them were blasted, some houses were half fallen by the strong blast. Wounded people were loitering here and there crying for help. There were few people who had not received wounds; I thanked God that I was safe.

And after thirty minutes' rest, I started again to ride on the way to the hill. It was about two o'clock; I felt I was hungry. When I was riding on I happened to see a certain house by the road. Abruptly I went into the gate without knowing who lived in it; a middle aged woman and a girl were there. There were also many refugees in every room. I explained to them how I had run away from the burning city and wanted to rest for a while; they led me in a room and served me kindly with cakes and tea. As I had some rice in my rucksack, I cooked it myself with potatoes which the woman gave me. After finishing lunch I said good-by to them and rode upon the hill again. On my way I saw lots of Navy trucks carrying many wounded people and dashing on the road of the hill to the north ward. The refugees were almost naked, their faces and hair were burned, and some were wearing bloody clothes, so I could not recognize whether they were

male or female.

Slowly a car came after me; I glanced in the car and saw a noble military officer lying with his wounded face bound up; afterwards I was told that he was a Korean Prince who was in the service of the Army; and he had received a serious wound near the Aioi Bridge, the centre of the atom falling on that day, when he was riding a horse, while his adjutant feeling his responsibilities that he was not near his master, committed suicide. On my way there was a primary school, many refugees gathered there and the wounded were receiving medical treatment and being served with hand-outs of biscuits or rice.

At this time the hill becoming steeper, I got down from my bicycle and began to walk. A truck filled with the wounded dashed on; when a woman's voice was heard from the truck calling my name,

"Mr. Ozaki! Mr. Ozaki!"

"Who are you?" I wondered

"I am Yamazaki, an official girl

of the Radio Station. I received a serious wound on my back." She said,

She was sitting in the middle of the seat wearing two simple pieces and having a sad countenance.

"Oh you are! Be careful of yourself. God will help you! About you I am sure to tell the manager. Please wait a bit."

The truck passed by and disappeared. As for her, she recovered after receiving medical treatment and is now working in our station.

I met two office-girls of our station on the way and one was walking with a stick as her foot was injured. I asked how they had run this way from the station; from it they had run to the River, after they crossed it in a boat just floating near they came this way crossing over the hill of Ushida. I congratulated them, and I parted with them as they were going to their friends' home near the village.

After one hour or so I came to the River and I had to cross it. There was a ferry-boat, being rowed by a boy.

He kindly took me and my bicycle on that boat. After I landed at the other side of the river, I requested him to tell me the fare,

"The fare? Do you think I can request money from the refugees? You have come from Hiroshima, I guess; from a refugee can I request money? Rather I must help you."

I was moved very much and I felt my eyes moistened. He knew how his comrades of this country were suffering from the disaster.

I came upon the bank. It was twilight. I asked some villagers the way to the Ifara Broadcasting Station and I was told I was in a twenty minute ride of it. A truck was dashing in the direction of Hiroshima, loaded with goods and rations; when it passed by me, some one in the truck threw something to me. I found it was some biscuits and I thanked them, as a heavenly gift. And six-thirty in the evening, safely I arrived at the station. There were already about ten of my co-workers who had reached there from the city and were waiting for the rest of workers to arrive. They were quite at a loss by the big event. The manager was there, and I explained to him all my experience in detail. The friends of the station welcomed me and gave me towels and other things - and served me a dish of warm rice and soup.

I discovered, though this station is about three miles away from Hiroshima, it had also received some damage by the atom-bomb having the window-glass on the roofs of the office broken by the blast. I understood how big the effect of the atom-bomb was. The station has a broad garden around the office. I went out in the garden, in the darkness I saw the flowers of bush-clover already beginning to bloom here and there in the garden. It was still, but on the southern sky about three miles beyond, I saw a great fire was still burning over the city fiercely and as brightly as day-time.

It is Hiroshima! our dearest city, our abode! I knelt down on the grass and prayed God for the safety of mother who was in our home and my only son named Sei-ichi who was working

in some factory near the city and my friends and their families who were not yet discovered by that time. Is this the end of Hiroshima? and the end of my life? I prayed; I felt God was helping me; in spite of calamity or misfortune God was still near me; there were some rooms to live in; some shelter to live in at some corner in this part of Japan. Disaster strengthened me. I remembered some verses from the scripture, -

"But we glory in tribulations also; knowing that tribulations worketh patience; and patience, experience; and experience, hope ---"

Yes! experience and hope! Cold wind awoke me from my meditations; I went in and prepared to sleep in the blankets on the hard floor. But I could not sleep a bit, and passed the night uneasy in mind and body.

III Chapter
Seeking after my Beloved ones.

"Obviously, circumstances alone do not make us happy or unhappy. Our feelings are determined by the way we react to them. We can all endure disaster and triumph over it — if we have to. We are stronger than we think."
—Dale Carnegie.

I got up with drowsy eyes. I felt dull in my body. Men in ordinary times can manage the right way, but on a different occasion, it is difficult to do the right way; an occasion may require; when people are at a loss facing disaster, they can't react against disaster. With the cold wind of the morning we came to ourselves, and the thought of the first step that we had to carry on, came across our minds. So the first step we had to do in the morning was to let our Tokyo Radio Station know our urgent event. The most of the trunk lines and other sending lines were cut by the blast; however we discovered there remained a line between Hiroshima

and Tokyo through Himeji City. So we sent a short report, saying "the city was destroyed by the attack of the planes, our station received fire, many deaths of workers, great fatal damage etc." There were lots of things to do about our station. But as I have mentioned before, all the sending lines and trunks line were destroyed, we decided, for the next step, to seek after the lost workers and families while we were waiting help from neighbor stations and Tokyo.

Therefore I left the station and began to ride on my bicycle to Hiroshima in order to seek after my family. The road to Hiroshima was so crowded with people, coming down and going to the city; wounded people, men carrying heavy rucksacks; cars, carriages and trucks jammed with refugees and things; some excited by the event, some drooping with fatigue and severe heat of summer, that it was very hard to ride. I came to Yokogawa, the entrance of the city. There was a truck full of food and relics; some one called me and gave me a hand out of rice. From here it became more difficult to ride on, because many electric poles, fallen houses and lots of timbers and break-stones stood on the way, the bridges were fallen and burnt. So I could not go to my home directly along the usual way. I had to go around the way, changing my course many times, sometimes crossing the smoking bridge; I stumbled frequently, but by all means I had to go to the West-bridge, near my home. I saw on the streets and in the rivers a great many corpses. On my way, near the West Telephoning Station, I heard very faint voices from an air raid shelter; I looked into it, and I discovered several naked girls wounded seriously and all their skin burnt, embracing each other; most of them seemed about to die already through moving somehow. I heard a girl with very weak voice, calling 'mother, mother' I asked her name but no reply. I could not extend help to them because there were no means to save them. Therefore I closed my eyes and prayed for them. Near by a certain woman with a baby in her hands was walking, full of tears. I understand the baby already has passed away.

At last I came to my home, near the Bridge and discovered it burnt to ashes.

This was my first experience in my life. I began to put away ashes and some breakstones and other metals, afraiding that somewhere under them the remains of mother would be found, when I heard a voice behind me, —

"Grand-ma is safe"

I was very much surprised to hear it. It was my son, safe and sound. We embraced each other in tears and thanked God. He explained as follows; when he had heard the sound of the bomb at the factory, he was knocked down by the blast, but not injured. He had run home in haste, which was within twenty minutes of the factory; when he had reached home our home was burning and grand-ma was standing at the gate with neighbors. He had found a carriage, then on it he put grand-ma and the neighbors and began to run away to the nearest village crossing the Bridge. He pulled on about twenty minutes or so, when a rescue truck happened to come and carried them to Jigozen fishing town about six miles away from the city. And they are now staying in a primary school.

I was very glad to hear my son's report and I immediately made up my mind to go there and see my mother. It was nearly evening when I reached Jigozen town on foot. The barrache of the school were jammed with the refugees. I found my mother resting on a mat at the corner of the ground, somehow excited and wounded in her left foot. She was very glad that I was safe.

Rice and soup were served for us, and clothes and shirts were donated to us. As the rooms of the school were crowded and some of the people were dying we decided to pass the night on the ground. But by the excitement of the event and stings of morquitoes we could not sleep well.

Chapter IV
The Burnt City

"By suffering men learn.
—Pascal

The 8th day of August came with shining

---

morning sun. I put my mother and son under the care of the officers in charge, saying good-by to them, because I had many, many things to do at the station.

I came to the centre of the city. Lo! It was a desert! (People were now calling it the Atom-desert), without inhabitants or trees, indeed no living ones; all the tram-cars had stopped being burnt here and there. The smell of the dead prevailed in the streets and in the air. The strong iron-concrete Aioi Bridge, near the centre of the atom-bomb was broken in some parts; the thick iron metal being bent and the wall of the bridge being blasted. I had heard about 200 workers of the Hiroshima Post Office were burned and died instantly on the mat, only two or three being saved; and about 600 officers of the Prefectural Government had the same fortune, too. All the passengers in a tram-car which happened to run near the centre died at one moment on that day! Indeed great sacrifice of humans and things in history.

I came in front of the Fukuya Department Store; gayish lights and cheerful chatterings of sales girls were no more;

smoking and burning only the outside concrete walls and floor remained. I came to the cross where there was the Kangyo Bank and there lots of seriously wounded citizens were lying on the floor of the bank. Most of them having the skin of their faces burned; all screaming and crying. Some physicians and nurses were helping them, binding the wounded spots or giving injections.

At last I came to our radio station. The new wooden office on the back ground was no more, but the main building was there. I entered it from the front gate; all the broadcasting machines and cabinets were broken, and the furniture, books, records, all gone to ashes. Water gushing out caused by cutting of pipes of water-supply and filled the room. I entered our room of Program Section; all changed into ashes except the metals; the room seemed to become broader than ever. I happened to find out a mess-tin, which I used to have before the fire, and I took it for a memorial. And next I went into the air-raid shelter; and found all the important things, personal and official, burnt or filled with water. I climbed up

to the top-roof of the station and looked around. It was a desert, nothing remained except some concrete building or half-burnt trees. The Hijiyama Hill was very near, it seemed.

On my way to the Hara Station I went to see the old Castle where the military base was. There was no more castle or military barracks. I found many soldiers' corpses lying in the drill ground and on the ponds around the old castle. The remains and stones of the castle or half-burnt trees only show the dreams of soldiers' past brilliant days. Militarism and feudalism were gone. I loitered for a while on the burnt grass and was recollecting on past days.

In the evening I returned to Hara Station. And we decided to borrow some farmer's room near the station for our workers. Though about thirty-five workers of our station died, it was fortunate all the secretaries of the Program Section were safe. Only some of them had received slight wounds and lost their wives or children.

About the great bomb which fell on Hiroshima there were lots of rumors, as I have mentioned before. G.H.Q of

Japan announced simply saying a great powerful scientific bomb fell on Hiroshima city, effecting great damage of persons and houses. Later we were told, by the information from U.S.A. it was the very atom-bomb that caused the big disaster, and we also understood for the first time that most of the dead or wounded were caused by radiation.

Rumors had spread that no living thing, human or trees, could live for seventy-five years in Hiroshima or the suburbs. So the refugees who remained in the broken houses or the air-raid shelter in the city began to remove to other parts of this country. To tell the truth, the percentage of the deaths increased; the citizens who had received radiation felt their hair began to drop out and some specks on the skin appeared; and they died day by day. Some died from infection resulting from the diminution of blood. Because all the crematoriums were destroyed, bereaved families of the city had to burn their dead beloved ones by themselves.

In a few days after the event of Hiroshima, the greatest events in the

world were the second atom-bomb fell at Nagasaki, and the Russian Declaration of war against Japan, as the Russian Army began to attack and invade the border-lines of Manchuria. Misfortune comes after misfortune. How could we sustain such a great attack? The last day of Japan was coming. The military and the navy had no power over Japan and the Japanese.

About this time, we are informed that Japan was negotiating peace with the Allied Forces. And later we were told that at noon sharp on August 15, some grave message would be announced by the Emperor, bidding that at that hour all the vehicles and cars should be stopped and hear the message. We were very busy to put this bulletin on the air. People in our country had waited impatiently and anxiously for this moment.

On that day, all the vehicles and men on the streets stopped and people in homes and offices listened eagerly to the radio. At first an announcer from Tokyo was introduced and we heard the voice of our Emperor and knew the last day of the War had come! But un-conditional surrender! I can't express the impression at that historical moment with a pen; how we felt and what would happen in this land afterwards. All wept; wept with mixed feelings respectively. All the service men were released and began to return from abroad. People who during the War, went to villages from cities, prepared to return to their homes or the burnt cities; all the rail-ways or ships or cars were jammed with these people; all taking large rucksacks with them, there was dis-order in the cars and in the streets for some period, until the Allied Forces arrived at this shore.

To tell of my personal matter, my mother who had returned to the city again and stayed in a half-broken house died in the early morning of September 1st because of the serious wound of her foot. I put fuel upon her body to set fire with my son! It seemed to be cruel to do so, but I could not help doing so, on that urgent occasion. God knows. In order to bury her remains, I was pre—

paring to go to my native country, Shikoku, over the Inland Sea, when a great flood came on September 17 midnight. Rains had lasted several days; at midnight I was awakened by the crying of someone "Flood! flood!" I opened the window; lo! the water was coming up to the second floor of the cottage where we were staying. If the house moved by the current of water what would happen? I saw on the cruel water, many logs and broken houses. We had no means to escape and so we only were waiting the decrease of water and the coming of daybreak. Luckily for us the water began to lower gradually with the coming of morning.

And by day breaking we felt we were safe; water dropped to about two feet. Flood after fire! By this damage of flood, collection of crops and vegetables would be decreased, it was announced. Our hearts were darkened.

As I had mother's remains with me, on that after-noon in the flood, I ventured with my son to go to the harbour which is about four miles south. And after much difficulty, crossing the currents of

flood many times. It was night when we came to the city; it was dark and a death-city without inhabitants; we found a broken tram-car and stayed in it about two hours, for rest; and started again to the harbour. Early the next morning we took a boat for my native country to bury the remains of my mother.

One day on a bright Autumn day of the year, soldiers of the Occupied Forces arrived at Kure, ex-naval port.
The new day had come!

V chapter
The Peace has come.

"We do not intend that the Japanese shall be enslaved as a race or destroyed as a nation, --- the Japanese Government shall remove all obstacles to the revival and strengthening of Democratic tendencies among the Japanese people.
— From Potsdam Declaration.

Four years have passed since the unforgettable day when the first atom-bomb fell on the land of Hiroshima. Now Japan where there is no more war, has started its first step as a nation of Democracy. All has changed! Feudalistic Japan has gone! The new Constitution of Japan was declared on November 3, 1947. And "freedom of speech, of religion, and of thought, as well as respect for the fundamental human rights" was established. Service men were released. All the soldiers abroad, from China, Siberia, and the South Seas have returned to their burnt and broken native places. Military and Navy were completely disarmed, while Japanese

Sovereignty was limited to the old islands, losing many of her colonies. In consequence, the population of the post-war of this country would become 80,000,000 people in the near future in this small area. On the other hand, the political and social conditions were in disorder for a while. With the inflation, daily living is becoming hard day by day; black-markets increased everywhere. Houses, food and clothes were few and the prices of them were becoming higher daily. Thieves, burglars, and murderers filled the cells of the police-stations. Uneasy days and restless nights have lasted long. Especially young folks who had received military education and training seemed to have lost their aim in life. And they also misunderstood the true meaning of Democracy; their way of life has become rough and disorderly, loitering in the streets or in the black-markets; or committing burglary in groups.

On book-stands, cheap, immoral books, magazines and printed

matter are selling, while house-wives had to go to the farms to buy rice, corn and vegetables from the farmer, exchanging for them their essential dresses.

Indeed Japan was in a crucible of disorder. But from the latter part of the third year, social conditions have become better in some degree; Allied Forces, especially U.S.A. and English, have extended their hands very much, food, clothes and other things were sent to this shore; Unrra and Lala goods are enlivening the orphans or widows or homeless folk; goods have increased, clothes were supplied, houses have been built.

Hope and reconstruction! We must carry on our new plans jer clem in spite of the disasters. In Hiroshima, at present we have 245,000 inhabitants (before the atom 312,200) and houses 60,000 (before the day 76,000). Department-stores, banks, cinema-show and the official and private organs have started their job; the tram-cars began to run; warm tea-rooms and nice cafes and restarants have opened their doors.

Ships full of cargo from abroad in

the harbour of Ujina; and foreigners are visiting daily to see the ruins of the Atom City, wondering how great the influence of the atom-bomb. Hiroshima is reviving. The campaign of "no more Hiroshimas" is now active in the world as well as in Japan.

Now we are echoing with joy and hope that "the Japanese people forever renounce war as a sovereign right of the nation and the threat or use of force as a means of settling international disputes" as the new Constitution of Japan declares to the peace-loving people. So it is not the last day of Hiroshima, but the first, hopeful day of it.
　　　　　　　— the End —

www.ingramcontent.com/pod-product-compliance
Lightning Source LLC
LaVergne TN
LVHW061227060426
835509LV00012B/1457